DAMAGED

Damaged relationships, damaged reputations,
damaged mental health

Prince Harry: A Case Study for Moral Injury and Posttraumatic Blame

Publications by Claire Carter:

Organisational injustice in UK Frontline Services and Onset of Post-Traumatic Embitterment Disorder (PTED), Moral Injury and PTSD - *International Journal of Law, Crime and Justice, Volume 66, September 2021, 100483* https://doi.org/10.1016/j.ijlcj.2021.100483

Overwhelming Injustice and Posttraumatic Blame Theory - Psychological wellbeing in frontline services (2020), ISBN-13:979-8667244325

Book review of Overwhelming Injustice and Posttraumatic Blame Theory, International Journal of Law, Crime and Justice, Dr Cody Porter - Volume 67, December 2021, 100492,
https://doi.org/10.1016/j.ijlcj.2021.100492

Duty of Care – Psychological Injury in Policing, Amazon, 2014, 2nd edition 2017

Publishing details:

ISBN: 9798379087180
Imprint: Independently published

About the Author

Claire has over 30 years' experience of working with people in multi-disciplinary teams and working alongside individuals within the health and social care environment. She has supported victims and survivors of Troubles-related terrorism in Northern Ireland. Her role has brought her up close to issues of transgenerational trauma and the direct impact of terrorism on physical and psychological injury and the continued wider effect on society. Claire was approached and encouraged to work in this role, after becoming well known within the policing community for her endeavours advocating for police officers with duty-related psychological injury. Her experiences in the role of charity founder and advocate to the policing family (at a time when there was no other support available), set her on the path of research into PTSD, Post Traumatic Embitterment Disorder

(PTED) and Moral Injury. Claire started the company, which later became the charity Safe Horizon UK, as a direct result of her former husband and police officer collapsing with complex PTSD, Anxiety and Depression. She was a full-time carer to him during several years of vulnerability and she herself was significantly affected by vicarious trauma (living alongside his symptoms). Her desire to support her husband and understand his condition spurred her on to seek others within the policing community affected by similar concerns. Claire had the privilege of being selected to meet with the Duke of Cambridge at the NPCC policing conference on mental health in September 2017. Claire has personal and professional experience developed over the last ten years, within the field of PTSD, vicarious trauma, chronic embitterment and Moral Injury, which has culminated in the publication of her research, and so that she may share her findings and knowledge with others more widely. As a result, Claire receives requests to peer review submissions on the subject of Moral Injury from Journals. Prior to this, Claire was employed in supported housing projects supporting victims and survivors of domestic abuse at high risk of violence and supporting ex-offenders.

Claire published her research 'Overwhelming Injustice and Posttraumatic Blame Theory' in 2020, as well as 'Organisational Injustice in UK Frontline Services and Onset of Post-Traumatic Embitterment Disorder (PTED), Moral Injury and PTSD' in 2021. Her research was peer reviewed by the International Journal of Law, Crime and Justice and received praise from professionals for her insights into this developing field of inquiry.

Contents

'Give me serenity to accept
what I can't change,
the courage to change what I can
and the wisdom to know the
difference'

Research method

The author has an objective view on Harry and Meghan, their relationship and their exit from the monarchy. She has never met either the Duke or Duchess of Sussex or read the press articles and social media posts about them prior to this research. However, she has a penchant for research into the subject of Moral Injury, Posttraumatic Blame theory and PTSD, and supporting people affected by often debilitating symptoms. What little she derived from television news broadcasts, since the launch of Harry's memoir 'Spare,' indicated he may be deeply troubled by chronic embitterment associated with these conditions. Hence her exploration into Harry and Meghan's story, as told by them.

The author has used primary sources for research purposes, taking care to avoid tabloid press articles where possible and to focus on Harry and

Meghan's own words. This is out of respect for Harry's intense negative feelings towards the Press, his statements that the Press print lies and the impact of Press opinions on his mental health. Furthermore, primary accounts are important for a baseline analysis of the Duke and Duchess of Sussex. The author has made conscious effort to concentrate on the words spoken by the Duke and Duchess of Sussex where possible. This includes their docuseries, TV interviews, interviews they have chosen to give to other media outlets and Harry's memoir 'Spare.' Harry emerged as someone quite unexpected, including the extent to which his mental health has been affected by trauma since the age of twelve and unresolved at the age of thirty-eight. At times the author was left confused by the contradictions within their story. Unable to answer the question of who are they, really? and instead focussing on what the evidence and facts suggest.

Preface

Harry was advised it would be very distressing to see the police file relating to his mother's car crash. Harry stated in his memoir 'Spare,'[1] *"Yes. I know. Sort of the point"* (p.106). This suggests Harry hoped viewing the file would be an antidote to his emotional numbing. He wanted to feel something - to cry. However, Harry's reaction to the photographic evidence he witnessed was rage. Harry did not apportion blame to his mother for not wearing a seat belt (which would have made the crash survivable), or for refusing her official security (the presence of which, would have prevented the crash). Harry did not blame the driver who was reportedly intoxicated with alcohol, mixed with prescribed drugs.[2] Perhaps because he was dead - could not be held accountable - could not be a target for Harry's

---

[1] (Mountbatten-Windsor, Spare, 2023)
[2] (Stern, 2022)

distress - 'look what you did to me, to my family, to all those who loved her' – instead blame was attributed to the British tabloid Press, for aggressively pursuing her and her vehicle. Immediately after her car crashed, while she lay injured and helpless on the back seat, paparazzi were photographing her. A photographer opened the car door and took pictures of her inside the car.[3] Harry stated, "*Not one of them was checking on her, offering her help, not even comforting her. They were just shooting, shooting, shooting...they'd also feasted on her defenceless body. The last thing Mummy saw on this earth was a flashbulb*" (p.107), not kindness, empathy, or humanity. However, paramedics reported she was conscious when they tended to her with medical care on route to the hospital.[4]

It could be reasonable to state Harry has a distorted perception of who was responsible for the traumatic event. The behaviour of the

---

[3] (Balakrishnan, 2008)
[4] (Batty, 2007)

4

paparazzi was a breach of Harry's values, morals, beliefs and expectations. One can speculate Harry wanted someone to blame who could be repeatedly punished publicly, which is a consequence of Posttraumatic Blame and Moral Injury. Harry has been at war with the Press ever since. The Press may have played a significant part in the tragedy and most certainly, their behaviour was repugnant, abhorrent and utterly disgraceful. Harry's reaction is understandable.

In an interview with Tom Bradby to promote his book 'Spare,' Bradby stated, *"by any account, this is an extraordinary tale and from your perspective, it's a holistic account of your life. This book takes things to a whole new level because it's a complete account of your life. However, I think I do have to start with a simple question, which is why, why have you written it?"*[5]

---

[5] (Mohan-Hickson, 2023)

Harry may speak of his lofty ideals and noble missions to reform the Press, reform the monarchy, tackle racism and unconscious bias, and to protect others (including younger generations of royals) - to speak his truth. However, these issues seem to deflect the observer away from his fundamental undeniable motivator - avoidance of environments that exacerbate his posttraumatic symptoms. Even as this book is under construction, Harry appears to seek a way out of returning to the UK for his father's coronation, stating he will only attend if he receives an apology from his father and brother, knowing the likelihood of an apology is slim. Harry largely achieved avoidance of the Press and royal life during military service and time spent out of the public eye in Africa and Australia. He continues to seek independence, autonomy and freedom from the monarchy. The only way this can happen, is if he can support himself financially and he has support from his wife to 'escape' his royal obligations and his home country.

Ironically though, Harry needs 'the fight' with the monarchy and the Press to generate public interest and sympathy, thereby generating an income stream. In a recent poll, only 21% of Britons surveyed believed Harry published his book to tell his side of the story.[6] This plan may not benefit Harry and Meghan in the longer term. Their recent disclosures – (a treachery and betrayal of the King), has seen their popularity plummet significantly. However, Britons overall still think the monarchy is good for Britain. [7] Harry achieved his objective with the publication of 'Spare.' The fastest selling non-fiction book since records began.[8] Harry was paid £20 million in advance of the book's release and for a four-book deal with the publisher Penguin Random House. He has donated $1,500,000 and a further

---

[6] (Morris & Smith, 2023)
[7] (Morris & Smith, 2023)
[8] (James, 2023)

£300,000 to charity from the proceeds of his memoir. [9] Harry and Meghan also earned approximately £100 million for a docuseries about their relationship.[10]

In addition to his desire for freedom and independence, Harry is determined to battle the organisational injustice and institutional betrayal he perceives. This is an indicator of Posttraumatic Blame and Moral Injury, which is a complication associated with PTSD. The result is the conflict between desire for avoidance and rumination on the injury. His relentless pursuit of vindication, to be 'right' in the eyes of the world,[11] has resulted in his 'tell-all' interviews and memoir, and multiple cases of litigation. Harry's accounts have generated gossip and sensationalism. This has in turn kept him in the Press and in the public eye – perhaps necessary evils to achieve his goals.

---

[9] (Ibrahim, 2022)
[10] (Kato, 2022)
[11] (Carter, 2020)

The publication of 'Spare,' the docuseries about the Duke and Duchess of Sussex and the TV interviews have been a quick way to earn big money, fast. This money was needed to support their independence and to pay for costly private protection services (p.387). Having no obvious skills, talents or trade, which Harry could apply to civilian life; Harry used the only currency he had. He sold his story. Harry and Meghan have betrayed the trust of close family members in the process. In some ways, they may have betrayed the British people too – shattering illusions and deeply held beliefs about the monarchy. The monarchy who should be beyond reproach and held to a higher standard than ordinary folk.

Harry and Meghan feel betrayed by the monarchy. Their expectation that protection would be provided, and funded by the institution was not met. This feeling of injustice is more pronounced because at the time the protection was withdrawn, Harry and Meghan perceived themselves and their son to be at significant risk of danger and harm. The dangers they identified were death threats, relentless public humiliation at the hands of the Press and the impact of Meghan's transition into the monarchy, which all had a significant impact on her mental health, including suicidal feelings.[12] Harry and Meghan appear to be both victims and perpetrators of Moral Injury.

There are many contradictions within the accounts given by Harry and Meghan – 'which are from their own lips.' These discrepancies perhaps prevent us from accepting their story as 'the truth.' Harry is determined that his is the only version of 'the truth. He stated, *"the only way he could protect his family was to correct mistruths, by writing the truth in one place* [his book]."[13] However, Harry does not explain what the alleged mistruths about him are. There are aspects of Harry's life previously unknown to the public, (some of which, could probably have remained so,

---

12 (Markle M. , 2021)
13 (Sabur & Nanu, 2023)

such as losing his virginity and developing frostnip on his penis...not to mention that he was thinking of his deceased mother when applying her brand of lip cream to his nether regions). Some clarity on which parts of the book specifically address mistruths would be beneficial. Harry makes vague accusations without substance. It seems he is trying to express a feeling, a perception and a sense of victimisation, rather than providing facts and evidence.

Harry's inability to consider other viewpoints and perceptions may indicate an embittered state of mind and lack of emotional intelligence.[14] What becomes apparent, is Harry's querulous self-righteous pursuit of revenge at all costs. For example, at the expense of his own popularity with the public and the loss of his family. The most worrying concern regarding Harry's state of mind, is his potential to destroy for no other

---

[14] (Carter, 2020)

reason than his self-absorbed, singular distorted perception of danger.

Harry appears to threaten in 'Spare' that he is not yet done with revenge and wants to feed on his family's fear and discomfort. He stated, an argument with his brother lasted over 72 hours. *"I saved the texts. I still have them"* (p.373). Harry stated he has a book deal to release further memoirs and he has material which his family would never forgive him for publishing.[15] The Duke stated, *"I love my mother country. I love my family. I just wish, at the second-darkest moment of my life, they'd both be there for me. They'll look back one day and wish they had too"* (p.386). One might venture, that Harry is blackmailing his family and holding them to ransom – this suggests Harry perceives himself as a victim, who has instead become the perpetrator - and his abuser has now become his victim. Where Harry once felt powerless and helpless, he now feels superior

---

[15] (James, 2023)

and powerful. The roles of victim and perpetrator have reversed.

Harry's posttraumatic perceptions, required a more sympathetic approach than rigid royal protocol provided. Perhaps if the Royal family had released statements in support of the Duchess of Sussex condemning abusive press, and if they had explained to Harry and Meghan that protection would be provided by security services on their visits to Great Britain (in addition to their own private security) where necessary, the current animosity may potentially have been avoided. It seems Harry sought reassurance. Instead, he was living in a constant state of hyperarousal. However, it may be possible that Harry and Meghan needed a 'bogeyman' to blame, in order to justify their departure from the monarchy to themselves and the world. In which case, there is nothing the Royal family could do to satisfy the Duke and Duchess then, now or in the future.

Perhaps Meghan would have received an abundance of positive coverage, if Harry had cooperated with the Press. It was within Harry's power to allow his wife to shine and for people to get to know her. However, he himself suppressed her voice and kept her at a distance from the Press. Did Harry manifest the danger to his wife (albeit unintentionally)? Perhaps the monarchy is not to blame for the conflagration.

It seems the monarchy could not understand Harry's posttraumatic symptoms and his need for safety strategies. And it seems Harry was unable to communicate his psychological injury. The miscommunication between Harry and the monarchy seems to have resulted in his feelings of victimization and need to reach out to the wider world for recognition. One might imagine Harry had normalised much of his thoughts, feelings and behaviours since his mother's death when he was twelve years of age. Therefore, he may not have recognised his need for help. But if Harry could not understand himself and his behaviour, how could his family possibly know what he needed?

In an interview, Harry stated *"one of the hardest bits which I realized pretty quickly was the moment that I started doing therapy. It's like we started speaking a different language. It just became very, very different. They wouldn't, they couldn't understand me and I was doing my best to try to encourage them to feeling. And everyone has their own journey, and I fully respect that. But within that institution* [the monarchy], *there is a mind-set. And there's a lot of people that are hired and brought in, that ultimately manage that mind-set. And I think it's really, really damaging and dangerous."*[16]

Harry appears frustrated by his inability to alter the perceptions of all those in his environment, to bring them in line with his own way of thinking and beliefs. Harry seems to seek affirmation from

---

[16] (Colbert, 2023)

the wider world that his beliefs and perceptions are in fact correct – that he is not paranoid or delusional. He attempts to garner sympathy and support from the public with his memoir and television interviews – to create the world in a way that makes him feel comfortable and stable. Harry's future orientation in life, may depend upon it. This is discussed further in the chapter on Moral Injury and Posttraumatic Blame.

Moral Injury and Posttraumatic Blame

SPARE is the Life Narrative of Prince Harry and a case study for Moral Injury (MI) and Posttraumatic Blame (PB). MI is a breach of one's expectations of self or others in accordance with roles and responsibilities, which challenges one's beliefs about safety, security and functional norms and leads to embitterment and blame.[17] MI can occur when there is a traumatic event and one attributes blame for the hurt, injustice or loss. Therefore, MI leads to PB.

Dr Jonathan Shay, who first identified MI in Vietnam veterans, believes the American Psychiatric Association (APA), responsible for the Diagnostic and Statistical Manual of Mental Health Disorders, has no appetite for recognising MI.[18] However, the author's own research found

---

[17] (Carter, 2020)
[18] (Shay, 2014)

that all symptoms associated with MI are already encompassed in the diagnostic criteria for PTSD.[19] Furthermore, the APA removed fear as the cause of PTSD in the fifth edition of the diagnostic manual (DSM-5). PTSD is no longer considered an anxiety disorder. This move is in recognition that the condition is caused by an external stressor (traumatic event),[20] thereby creating space for Moral Injury to be attributable to the onset of PTSD.

PTSD treatment has proved ineffective for many individuals. Research suggests addressing MI may support successful PTSD treatment.[21] Understanding MI could improve PTSD recovery, as well as help people to overcome traumatic experiences, which feature an element of betrayal, injustice or wrongdoing - rather than focus solely on fear and anxiety.

---

[19] (Carter, 2021)
[20] (American-Psychiatric-Association, 2020)
[21] (Koenig, 2019)

Perhaps the most significant symptoms of MI identifiable in the DSM-5 diagnostic criteria for PTSD; are criteria D2: Persistent and exaggerated negative beliefs or expectations about oneself, others or the world - for example, Harry's belief he and his wife are in mortal danger because of the Press and that in relation to Princess Diana, history will repeat itself with Meghan. He believes his family are collaborating with the enemy (the Press) at the expense of his own interests and to portray him and his wife in a negative light; and D3: Persistent, distorted cognitions about the cause or consequences of the traumatic event (s) that lead the individual to blame self or other[22] - for example, Harry's belief the Press were responsible for his mother's death. Had they assisted her immediately after the car crash, perhaps the outcome would have been different. He roundly blames the Press for her death.

---

[22] (Carter, 2021)

MI can coincide with a traumatic event. For example, the traumatic incident may involve a moral wrongdoing, an injustice or betrayal by someone in a trusted position. [23] This could include the response from others to the trauma, such as blaming the victim or collusion with the perpetrator. [24] Harry believes his family are colluding with the perpetrator (tabloid press) in exchange for gaining positive press coverage.

Trust in people can be lost when they behave in a way that breaches the expectations of their role at work or in society. [25] This is perhaps more significant when the perpetrator of the MI is responsible for one's safety and welfare, such as a parent, care giver, partner, spiritual or religious figure, employer, workplace supervisor, judicial system, government or statutory agency. Harry perceives the Royal family to have power over the Press and the power to provide protection from

---

[23] (Shay, 2014)
[24] (Freyd & Smith, 2013)
[25] (Linden & Maercker, 2011)

abusive articles. Yet he contradicts this assertion by stating Queen Elizabeth II was unable to help. Her hands were tied. [26] Furthermore, that the Duke and Duchess of Sussex should have protection from British security services full-time, after abdicating from royal duties and emigrating. However, Harry's beliefs were shattered when he was forced to arrange privately funded security once he stepped back as a senior working royal.[27]

A person's beliefs about other people, oneself or the world are undermined when a moral code is broken. One may blame themselves for failing to prevent what happened. The injured person is left feeling unsafe and insecure, and may feel the world and their place in it no longer makes sense. They can become stuck in a state of emotional distress.[28] Harry berated himself for putting his wife in a position of danger. He has had to find a

[26] (GMA, 2023)
[27] (Swift, 2022)
[28] (Carter, 2020)

way to survive outside the protection, direction and confines of both the monarchy and the military. He has perhaps lost much of his self-identity and is in the process of re-creating himself. Yet, he cannot let go of past hurt and humiliation. Rather than focus on the future with his family, he is determined to focus on his feelings of victimisation.

MI shares the same symptoms as Complex PTSD (such as, feelings of anger, blame, guilt, shame, persistent negative beliefs about oneself or others, and difficulty with relationships).

These symptoms can result in feelings of humiliation, injustice, betrayal, loss of trust, difficulty with forgiveness, revenge fantasy, loss of faith, loss of meaning and purpose in life, embitterment and fluctuation between rumination on what happened and avoiding painful memories or reminders. Rumination (thinking about the event over and over again), is a significant symptom of MI.[29] Rumination on a grudge sees ones' 'physical arousal soar', such as increased heart rate and blood pressure and emotional reactions such as anxiety, sadness and anger, which can arouse and maintain symptoms of PTSD, thereby rendering treatment ineffective.[30]

People more likely to develop MI, are perhaps those who hold rigid perceptions, strict principles and beliefs, high expectations and consider themselves self-sacrificing. [31] Harry describes himself as someone who served his Queen and country, and who was prepared to die for them both (p.6-7) Harry stated *"having spent ten years in the army I learnt a specific set of values, and if I see wrongdoing, I will be lured towards trying to resolve it. if I can't continue to serve my country while based in the UK, for numerous different*

---

[29] (Carter, 2020)
[30] (Linden & Maercker, 2011) (Worthington, 2004)
[31] (Linden & Maercker, 2011)

reasons, one because of lack of security, then I will continue to serve my country from abroad."[32]

Cynicism and suspiciousness may also be contributing factors. [33] Harry describes his suspicions of people around him, leaking information to the enemy (the Press).

Feeling hopeless and powerless are features of MI, which leads to a sense of victimisation. However, Harry too, has leaked private moments and conversations, creating cynicism and suspiciousness in others. He is no longer thought of as trustworthy.

As long as humanity exists, morally injurious acts will occur. They have done so throughout history. Dr Jonathan Shay (father to the concept of MI), demonstrates this with great success in his books 'Achilles in Vietnam' [34] and 'Odysseus in America.'[35] He acknowledges other definitions of

---

[32] (Mohan-Hickson, 2023)
[33] (Linden & Maercker, 2011)
[34] (Shay, 2003)
[35] (Shay, 2002)

MI have since been proposed, to include witnessing, failing to prevent or perpetrating a moral transgression. However, he is emphatic that MI features a failure of someone with legitimate authority to do what's right in a high-risk situation. [36] An example, could be Harry's perception the Press did nothing to help his mother immediately after the car crash, and the monarchy did nothing to protect his wife from Press vitriol. Arguably, we all have a reasonable understanding of societal norms, expectations and decency. Yet, morals are also dependent on personal values and beliefs, and an individual's perception of an event.[37] This may complicate the matter of judgement. Harry acknowledges the variance in perception between himself and his family.[38]

---

[36] (Shay, 2014)
[37] (Barnes, Hurley, & Taber, 2019)
[38] (Colbert, 2023)

Corruption, collusion, duress and incompetence could lead to morally injurious behaviour. Punishment for the harm cannot undo the damage once done. Indeed, many people are unsatisfied with the outcome of justice, because the injury and loss remain. What is perceived as immoral behaviour by one person may be considered justified and reasonable by another.[39] The monarchy, (an institution which, has survived over one thousand years) considers their actions reasonable, proportionate and compliant with predetermined rules and protocols. Principles important to one individual may be of no consequence to someone else. Harry has no regard for tradition, rules, or conformity (p.36, p56). This challenges how we view the idea of moral wrongdoing, accountability and responsibility.

---

[39] (Carter, 2020)

Psychological injury may lead to persistent, distorted perceptions about the cause of the injury, or of others and the world in general.[40] Some might say there is paranoia that comes with distrust. While this may be true, it is perhaps important to suggest that cynicism and suspiciousness may be based on real experience. Someone familiar with danger, may see threats that are not there, or they may observe potential danger, which is distorted. It is paradoxical that two people exposed to the same event, at the same point in time and in the same space; can experience the incident differently. We create our own perception. Harry stated, "*I think what will be quite shocking or surprising to people is that after our mother died, [my brother and I] were on different paths. Two individuals who experienced a very similar traumatic experience, but dealt with it in two very different ways.*"[41]

---

[40] (Carter, 2021)
[41] (Mohan-Hickson, 2023)

People in positions of power and authority, should strive to meet the expectations of their role. Individuals should be prepared for the fact that their expectations of others may not be fulfilled. It is wise to consider the adage that one cannot control the behaviour of others. One can only control how they choose to respond. Of all the thoughts, feelings and behaviours associated with MI - blame and difficulty with forgiveness are perhaps the most significant.

Blaming oneself for failing to protect others or prevent what happened can lead to difficulty with forgiveness too. Embitterment can be pleasurable, painful and addictive. People are not sure if they want to heal.[42] Chemicals released in the body, when living in a state of crisis can be addictive, and provide relief from boredom. This can lead people to ruminate on the trauma or repeatedly seek traumatic experiences. [43] This could explain (in part) hostility towards the idea

---

[42] (Linden & Maercker, 2011)
[43] (Bessel-Van-Der-kalk, 2015)

of forgiveness and 'moving on.' Harry has stated he is not sure if he will forgive his family or the Press (p.455).

The author posits that MI could lead to Posttraumatic Blame, which is a theory published in her research in 2020.[44] For PB to apply there must be a traumatic incident, for which one perceives a person(s) or organisation to be responsible for the injury or loss suffered. The individual assesses the traumatic event and the participants involved (including self). One may question whether the incident and the consequences could have been prevented. Was there negligence? Was this intentional? Did those involved have the capacity to prevent what happened? For example, did they have mental, emotional and physical capability, or practical and material resources? Did they have the knowledge or experience, which meant they should have known better or done better?

---

[44] (Carter, 2021)

Blame is attributed if someone is perceived to be responsible and accountable. An injustice or wrongdoing has occurred – the perception of which shatters previously held beliefs about life, people or systems.

The disruption to deeply held values and norms disorientates the individual and affects one's ability to visualize or plan for the future. The individual may wonder how they will be able to exist in a world which does not share their values (as they once believed). An unimagined future, results in a loss of meaning, purpose and motivation in life. Anhedonia (loss of pleasure or enjoyment) may be attributed to this loss of orientation. One becomes locked in a mental and emotional state of distress. Thoughts and feelings are in disarray as one attempts to make sense of the traumatic incident. This may include why and how this happened, processing loss and grief, coming to terms with a significant life change and feelings of vulnerability or insecurity.

Harry stated he felt lost and hopeless. He turned to alcohol and illicit drugs in response. He struggled to find his own identity, meaning and purpose in life, until joining the military.

One may attempt to organize thoughts and feelings about what happened, through a process of replaying memories of the event. The aim is to reach an understanding, to solve problems, or determine a course of action. The goal of the individual is to regain a sense of personal control, security, safety and future direction. However, highly charged emotions may result in unhelpful rumination rather than solution-focused reflection.

One may become driven to seek justice, to the exclusion of other important areas of life. The persistent pursuit for 'justice' can affect relationships, work life, finances and security. However, the need to reassert one's beliefs about how people and the world should operate or behave - to re-establish beliefs which were shattered may seem to outweigh the risks. Justice may not be forthcoming and even if achieved, cannot undo what has happened. The persistent pursuit of justice can entrench and exacerbate symptoms by keeping the memory of the event alive.

Harry has instigated multiple cases of litigation and is demanding accountability from the Royal family – He appears to try reinstating shattered beliefs regarding his entitlement to provision of security services and that the level of danger towards him is high. Regarding the Press, he seeks revenge for his mother's death and sets out to destroy them as an institution. Regarding the monarchy, Harry resents the royal life he felt he had no choice in, which significantly affected his young life. Since meeting Meghan, Harry feels enabled to finally tackle the injustice he perceives.

Symptoms of PB are predominantly anhedonia, future disorientation, embitterment, rigid perceptions, anger and persistent desire for justice, which may be disproportionate to the offence. Naturally, other symptoms occur as a result, such as persistent negative beliefs about others (distrust), guilt, shame and un-forgiveness.

PB can lead to unacceptance, a focus on anger and action directed to others (which may include desire for revenge), or grief, sadness and feelings of victimization. One may be resistant to change.

The goal is for the individual to reach a new understanding of the world; and adapt to new beliefs and way of life. Then one can assimilate the traumatic experience into this altered view. Harry is still trying to convert his family and the world to his perception and has not yet adapted to his new world order.

Harry assessed the traumatic event (his mother's death). He considered the Press capable of assisting his mother and negligent to do so.

Blame was attributed to the British tabloid Press. His beliefs about humanity and decency were shattered. Harry continues to try and restore his shattered beliefs through the pursuit of justice, litigation and social action. His predominant trait is rage, anger and action directed at others (not sadness or grief). Harry is perhaps right to use his experiences to fight for the benefit of others, so they need not endure the same treatment. However, it is important to undertake this work with wisdom and Posttraumatic Growth at the heart of all action; not bitterness, vengeance or anger (which are the hallmarks of a perpetrator of abuse).

Harry's break with the monarchy – his new life and pursuits in America, seem to be an attempt to carve out an alternate existence for himself. However, his reliance on the press and media (a re-traumatizing factor in his life) remains at this time. After abdicating from his royal duties, and leaving the UK for privacy, Harry instigated the release of his 'tell-all' book 'Spare,' TV docuseries about the Duke and Duchess of Sussex and TV and press interviews. Whether for catharsis, for money, or to publicly humiliate others (and seek revenge), the fact is Harry has not yet succeeded in ending his relationship with publicity and the press, which could perhaps be necessary for recovery. In his memoir 'Spare,' Harry confirms the affliction of post-traumatic stress began with his mother's death in 1997, and his most significant symptom is his fear of cameras (p.225). He also refers to himself as avoidant, anxious, agoraphobic and suffering panic attacks (p.253). With this in mind, Harry will need to adopt coping strategies to help him manage the inevitability of cameras as a public figure. The Press are challenged to approach future interactions and coverage, in a way that does not deliberately exacerbate his condition unnecessarily. The question is, can Prince Harry heal and recover from entrenched symptoms associated with PTSD, MI and PB.

Context

"I was all about She-Ra, Princess of Power, a sword-wielding royal rebel - not Cinderella."
(Meghan Markle, 2014)

Harry was 'spare to the heir.' There was an expectation that should his brother (the future King) die, he would take up the mantle. Harry bitterly complains of feeling unfairly treated as the 'Spare,' and of sibling rivalry. Harry stated with resentment and an air of superiority that, *"Willy was at Sandhurst too now. A fellow cadet. (He'd started after me, because he'd gone to university first.) He couldn't resort to his typical attitude when we were sharing an institution, couldn't pretend not to know me—or he'd be insubordinate. For one brief moment, Spare outranked Heir"* (p.115). Harry sarcastically stated, *"I was the Plan B. I was brought into the world in case something happened to Willy. I was summoned to provide backup and, if necessary, a spare part. Kidney, perhaps. Blood transfusion.*

Speck of bone marrow. This was all made explicitly clear to me from the start of life's journey and regularly reinforced thereafter" (p.15). The bitterness and cynicism are evident in Harry's tone.

Prince William's children became next in line to the throne, superseding Harry once they were born, which further diminished Harry within the hierarchy of the Royal family. On a balance of probability, Harry would no longer be required as 'Spare to the Heir,' since the birth of Prince George nine years ago, yet he chose 'Spare' as the title for his memoir – perhaps an identity he has not relinquished in his own mind. However, Harry does not demonstrate the makings of a King throughout his book, nor a desire to burden this responsibility.[45] He should perhaps feel grateful or relieved he was not first born, as his character and the values he holds, are not in keeping with the expectations of a monarch.

---

[45] (Mohan-Hickson, 2023)

He contradicts his grievance of unfair treatment, when he recounts the love and affection he received from family members, his special treatment from Queen Elizabeth II (p.332) and the public's continued affection for him as 'the naughty one' (p.222).

Prince Harry, Duke of Sussex, stated his memoir 'Spare' and the accounts of his life shared during his TV interviews are *"my words from my lips,"*[46] which dispels any notion of Harry as misrepresented or misquoted by the ghost writer of his autobiography. An autobiography he would have reviewed and approved prior to publication.

Ironically, Harry stated *"Mummy's former butler had penned a tell-all, which actually told nothing. It was merely one man's self-justifying, self-centering version of events. My mother once called this butler a dear friend, trusted him implicitly. We did too. Now this. He was milking her for money"* (p.89). Harry's memoir 'Spare,' is also a tell-all,

---

[46] (Mohan-Hickson, 2023) (Colbert, 2023)

self-justifying, self-centred version of events with no substance, published to make money, at the expense of his family's trust. Harry does not appear to recognise his hypocrisy in publishing his book for self-serving reasons. His behaviour is arguably no better than that of Diana's former butler.

For those with a keen interest in Moral Injury, embitterment and Querulous behaviour, Harry's memoir and interviews offer a treasure trove of anecdotes on his experience as a victim and a perpetrator. Harry fights for his right to privacy, yet 'Spare' is perhaps a disclosure of 'too much information.' Furthermore, Harry does not spare other people within the book with a respectful silence. Instead, he tells the world of private conversations and interactions with family, friends and past lovers. It is not clear whether Harry sought their permission to publish such intimacies. Did Harry breach their trust?

Harry stated, people *"said I only pretended to want privacy, said Meg was pretending as well"* (p.310). Harry stated, *"whenever I complained about it, privately or publicly, people just rolled their eyes. They said I was whingeing. Wah-Wah give us a break."* This was followed by victim blaming such as *"she's used to [paparazzi], in fact she wants them"* (p.310).

Privacy means respectful boundaries and consent to what is shared, when, where and how often. Diana stated in an interview that the paparazzi and media attention was overwhelming. She understood she would receive Press attention when on Royal duties. However, the Press intrusion was there every time she left her front door. [47] Privacy does not equate to complete media blackout – it means individuals have the right to share some of themselves, some of the time and they have a right not to have their private lives constantly invaded.

---

[47] (Sussex, 2022)

Harry is accused of Whingeing. Moaning and relentlessly offloading bitterness onto others is synonymous with MI and PB. Friends and family can disappear when their tolerance expires. They may implore the individual to 'let go' and 'move on.' However, this is not the goal. The aim is to understand why or how this is happening, learn from the event, safeguard self from a repeat experience and safeguard others from the same peril. Harry clearly sets out to achieve this, by telling his story, challenging the Press through litigation and holding the monarchy accountable. However, this does not excuse acting without the express permission or consent of others in relation to their own affairs, or betraying the trust of others to achieve this aim. One must be mindful not to become a perpetrator of injury, in the pursuit of remedying one's own victimhood. Furthermore, the Duke and Duchess are sending conflicting messages with attention seeking behaviour.

Harry's brother, on the other hand, has maintained a dignified silence, which Harry may be relying on – knowing the future king is highly unlikely to risk the reputation of the monarchy by retaliating, or presenting the Press and the public with a different version of events. Journalists suggest Prince William was of significantly less interest to them than Prince Harry. William didn't provide opportunities to sensationalize stories about him, which would sell papers.[48] But Harry, stated he sometimes "asked for it" and gave the Press what they wanted (p.358). Is Harry partly responsible for a situation he created and then complained about?

Harry seems to experience symptoms of posttraumatic stress, Posttraumatic Blame and Moral Injury. Can his behaviour towards the Press, and his kith and kin be excused, or his accountability diminished? Is his behaviour driven by distorted perceptions, rage, paranoia,

---

[48] (Rajan, 2021)

delusion, danger seeking, recklessness, self-destructive actions or poor decision making?

Now Harry has said his piece – it is perhaps time to retreat from the public eye (a re-traumatizing factor) - a time of reflection, allowing the dust to settle and channelling energy into reconciliation with his family. Unfortunately, Harry has breached their trust with his memoir. Once trust is broken, it can be nigh-on impossible to retrieve it. Harry has demonstrated his willingness to share family secrets for the right price, just as Meghan's father sold a 'private' letter and photographs to the Press for money too (p.356). Harry has provided the media with an abundance of material, by which they can criticize and ridicule him with the publication of 'Spare.' As well as TV docuseries, and TV and Press interviews. Perhaps Harry would be advised to end his addiction to the media in pursuit of the normality, freedom and privacy, which he states he has always sought and found in some private corners of the world.

Harry stated "if *there was one thing to which, I did seem undeniably addicted, however, it was the Press. Reading it, raging at it. [The therapist] said these were obvious compulsions*" (p.312). Harry is still at war, though he refutes this. He holds onto the past and what happened because he feels he must. He stated he is not stuck in the past and he will never be stuck.[49] Yet, he feels that letting go of the pain and anger will amount to forgetting his mother. This keeps the Moral Injury alive and his symptoms of posttraumatic stress in a state of arousal. It seems Harry has chosen the path of embitterment instead of wisdom. It is his anger and pain that drives his relentless pursuit of justice, not Posttraumatic Growth and the wisdom to acknowledge the good which has already been achieved as a result of his mother's tragic death and his life's journey so far – such as reform of the Press Complaints and Press regulatory bodies, which now protect everyone from harm (including victims of crime). Or the

---

[49] (Mohan-Hickson, 2023)

meaning and purpose he has found in helping veterans through the Invictus Games. Or changes in legislation protecting the privacy of VIPs and celebrities in places like California and the UK. This may be because of his negative self-concept and lack of self-esteem, which he speaks of throughout 'Spare.' Instead, Harry places Meghan on a pedestal – he sees her as smarter, more dynamic, more accomplished. In the process, he undermines his own achievements and the difference he has made to the lives of many disadvantaged people. His low self-esteem may feed his addiction to the Press and media attention – perhaps this is the only place he feels of worth, and can compete with his wife's 'dizzying CV' (p.272).

Unless someone experiences symptoms of anxiety, posttraumatic stress, Moral Injury and other psychological injuries (or lives intimately alongside these symptoms) – understanding the rationale behind the individual's behaviour can be difficult. The person may struggle to understand their own behaviour, so trying to explain their needs to someone else can be problematic. This can lead to miscommunication, misunderstanding, tension, isolation, withdrawal from others and the breakdown of important relationships.

Harry acknowledged he had some responsibility for the breakdown in his relationship with the monarchy.[50] His relationship with Meghan and starting therapy 7 years ago were the catalyst for his self-exile in 2020. However, it seems Harry and Meghan needed to direct blame elsewhere for their decision to leave the Royal family and the UK. Perhaps to ease feelings of guilt or shame. Therefore, it seems the monarchy and the Press became scapegoats.

When cross-referencing the oral accounts made by Harry and Meghan during interviews, with the memoir 'Spare,' discrepancies come to light. This has provoked a need to understand the

---

[50] (GMA, 2023)

underlying values driving the decisions and the behaviour of the Duke and Duchess. Why did they *really* abdicate as senior royals? Harry stated during a TV interview that Meghan was always going to leave. [51] However, when asked if she calculated their exit from the monarchy, manipulated the circumstances to this end, and had planned to exploit the monarchy to build her brand, Meghan stated *"I left my career, my life. I left everything because I love him, and our plan was to do this [royal life] for ever."* However, *"74,000 articles had been published about Meghan worldwide since the duke and duchess confirmed plans to distance themselves from the palace. On top of this, searches for the duchess jumped 600% after the Oprah interview was announced."* [52] Whether unintentional or by design, the abdication of the Duke and Duchess from Royal duties has certainly raised Meghan's public profile and earned her a place in the history

---

[51] (Colbert, 2023)
[52] (Taylor, 2021)

books. For some people, there is no such thing as 'bad PR' (public relations). It is hard to imagine Meghan would suffer any financial, social or vocational detriment if her marriage dissolved. Whereas, Harry could be left completely out in the cold. Their relationship certainly seems to be one of interdependency at this time. However, if Harry's behaviour affects Meghan's reputation in society or her own psychological health, this could create strain on the relationship.

Harry indicates that he saw Meghan as a way out of the monarchy and to finally find the freedom and independence he had always wanted. When asked *"Do you think you would have left or ever stepped back were it not for Meghan?"* Harry replied *"No. The answer to your question is no."* He stated, *"I wouldn't have been able to [leave], because I myself was trapped. I didn't see a way out."*[53] In relation to his wife as an actor, Harry

---

[53] (Markle M., 2021)

stated, "*some kinds of fame provide extra freedom, but royal fame was fancy captivity*" (p.199).

Harry maintains "*I didn't know I was trapped.*" However, he writes of his desire for freedom and normality occurring before he met his wife, and from a young age. For example, when spending time in Africa, Australia and the military – he drew comparisons between life as a Royal and an existence where his status meant nothing. Harry identified a yearning for life away from the pressures and restrictions of the monarchy. He had escaped much of Royal life when he spent ten years in the military. Sadly, for Harry, his time in the armed forces came to an end in 2015 and he was faced with a transition into a quasi-civilian life. Something all veterans can have difficulty with. He stated, "*from now on I'd be something I'd never been: a full-time royal. How would I even do that? And was that what I wanted to be?*" (p.247).

It is easy to fathom that Harry would seek a life partner who could offer him an escape route. A non-conformist, an independent woman, a person not of the aristocracy and a woman used to being in the public eye. Someone who would not be comfortable within the confines and restrictions of the Royal family. A woman who could handle the Press. A partner with an entrepreneurial spirit to support them financially as a family.

Harry stated he understood his former partner's desire for freedom and that if he had a choice, he would not have chosen his life within the monarchy (p.156).

He was desperate to marry and to be a father, but he needed a partner capable of coping with the scrutiny from the Press (p.155). Harry stated "*I saw the pain and suffering of women marrying into this institution." How can I ever find someone willing and capable to withstand all the baggage that comes with being with me? I was terrified*

[Meghan] *would be driven away by the media."*[54] Harry felt the pressure of finding a suitable love match to wed. He stated, *"As a confirmed bachelor I was an outsider, nonperson within my own family. I wanted that to change, I had to get hitched, which made my twenty-ninth birthday a complex milestone"* (p.231). *"Maybe if I get married, things will be different?"* (p.238).

Things certainly were different after his marriage and worsened his relationship with his family.

The Royal Editor to the Sunday Times stated she had a good working relationship with Harry around the time of his Invictus games (2016). He was in a good place in his life. He was open and honest. Harry was concerned he would not find a partner who could endure the Press attention and invasion of privacy. It seems Harry manifested his own desires in Meghan Markle who he then met in 2016.

---

[54] (Sussex, 2022)

He speaks of his frustrations throughout 'Spare,' including the difficulty with relationships before meeting Meghan. When Meghan reciprocated his desire to pursue a relationship, he saw an opportunity to escape his *'gilded cage.'* He stated she was as free as a bird (p.269). However, there is no evidence to suggest this was a conscious strategy. Rather the subconscious needs to align one's environment with one's desires.

Harry and Meghan also stated they would have stayed within the Royal family if they had received help and support.[55] However, Meghan stated in an interview *"Yes, I think everyone welcomed me."*[56] Harry speaks at length of the kindness shown to Meghan by his family and how she was very much included. It seems the real reason for their departure was not a lack of support. It was their own difficulty meeting the job specification.

---

[55] (Markle M. , 2021)
[56] (Sussex, 2022)

The two lifestyles (independence and self-serving behaviour - versus devoted servitude and sacrifice) are incompatible. Harry stated, *"we always wanted to continue to serve, we just didn't want to be based and living in the UK all the time. One of the main reasons for that was to remove ourselves from this competition that was happening for the front pages,"* [57] indicating competition for the limelight was intolerable and the Duke and Duchess would have greater autonomy away from the Royal household.

Harry stated, *"Camilla had sacrificed him on her "personal PR altar", "She had a reputation to rehabilitate. She's someone who married into this institution and done everything she can to improve her own reputation, her own image, for her own sake."*[58] Harry does not appreciate Camilla may have benefitted from positive press coverage, which she earned on her own merit and through her good works. Nor does he consider Meghan

---

[57] (Mohan-Hickson, 2023)
[58] (GMA, 2023)

may have married him to secure status and publicity for herself. Meghan has not been particularly successful or 'made it big' in any of her ventures. Meghan appears to be a socialite, who focuses on networking and befriending high profile celebrities. She also uses the celebrity status and profile of others to promote her own public image. For example, interviewing people with status for her (now archived) lifestyle blog or 'Archetypes' podcast. One such archived interview with Princess Alia (Libyan royalty), dated 7th July 2014, caught the attention of the media.

Meghan reportedly stated *"Little girls dream of being princesses. I, for one, was all about She-Ra, Princess of Power. For those of you unfamiliar with the '80's cartoon reference, She-Ra is the twin sister of He-Man and a sword-wielding royal rebel known for her strength. We're definitely not talking about Cinderella here."* [59] The articles suggest Meghan

[59] (Sangster, 2023) (Crawford-Smith, 2023) (Galpin, 2023)

Markle had fantasized about being a princess since childhood and identified her own archetype as She-Ra, 'Royal Rebel' prior to meeting Prince Harry – with predetermined intentions to shake-up the monarchy. However, when accessing the archived Tig article, on 19th February 2023, it states, *"little girls dream of being princesses. I, for one, was all about She-Ra, Princess of Power. And grown women seem to retain this childhood fantasy. Just look at the pomp and circumstance surrounding the royal wedding and endless conversation about Princess Kate. So, when my dear friend, Misan Harriman, introduced me to Princess Alia Al Senussi, I had a bit of a "pinch-myself-I'm-emailing-with-a-princess" moment. The Al Senussi family was exiled from Libya when Gadhafi seized the throne in a coup d'état. But that hasn't stopped Alia from flexing her respective royal muscle. Alia is on the Board of Trustees for Global Heritage Fund, where she concentrates on their activities in Libya."*[60] It appears some of the

---

[60] (Markle, 2014)

content has been removed since the articles were published, because the words were quoted, not paraphrased or implied. Princess Alia appears to be a potential role model for Meghan – exiled, yet still titled and able to use her status for high profile positions on the world stage – still able to 'flex her royal muscles.' It's as if Meghan has infiltrated the monarchy, secured her royal titles through marriage, created a scenario by which she and her husband would be forced to exile (immediately after she bagged the princess title and beget the son and heir), make millions of dollars, secure a place in history and raise her profile. Then return to an environment where she can reap all those rewards as a staunch feminist living independently in modern society. If this were true, that would be a strategic move and a rather impressive achievement.

Meghan and Harry may announce dedication to a life within the monarchy and an intention to continue as working senior royals. However, the fact is, one cannot maintain the pretence of living someone else's values indefinitely. People always revert to type. Harry stated *"We were dedicated to a life of service, as is proven by everything that we're doing now with the work that we do. We can't cope in this situation and we're going to put our mental health first."*[61]

Even if the Duke and Duchess of Sussex had the best intentions to meet the expectations of others, with the best will in the world they could not sustain the royal way of life. Imagine Meghan asking an ancient, historical institution over a thousand years old, to change its rules, protocols, attitudes and 'way of doing things' to appease her (as an individual). This would surely be a delusion of grandeur and narcissistic trait.

Difficulties arose immediately after the wedding and once Meghan's marriage was secured. There were reports of staff at the palace being bullied by Meghan, which led to some people leaving.

---

[61] (Mohan-Hickson, 2023)

Meghan threatened the news reporter with legal action for publishing this claim. However, she never took this any further, presumably because there was evidence to support the bullying allegations and Meghan knew a court case would backfire and damage her reputation.[62]

In an interview, Meghan stated she had lost her career, her independence and her voice, since becoming a Royal. She was micro-managed, stifled, isolated, lonely and trapped. The situation was untenable for her. Meghan stated, *"I've always worked. I've always valued independence. I've always been outspoken, I've advocated for so long for women to use their voice, and then I was silent."* She stated she was silenced.[63]

However, Vanity Fair stated *"The Queen is remarkably open-minded and she's very tolerant, William was allowed to cohabit with Kate (Middleton), even though she's the daughter of a*

---

[62] (60-minutes-Australia, 2022)
[63] (Markle M. , 2021)

very middle-class family. The Queen just looked at who Kate was and that she was in love with her grandson, and that she knew how to conduct herself with dignity and discretion, and that was the most important thing."[64] What Meghan refers to as being silenced is perhaps what the Royal family would refer to as exercising discretion and dignified silence.

The list of charitable work and patronage undertaken by members of the Royal family is extensive. Since becoming the Duchess of Sussex and a senior working royal, Meghan became spokesperson and advocate for the Association of Commonwealth Universities (ACU), The National Theatre, Smart Works – which *"exists to help long term unemployed and vulnerable women regain the confidence they need to succeed at job interviews, return to employment and transform their lives,"* and the Mayhew animal welfare

---

[64] (Kashner, 2017)

charity. [65] She also attended many events worldwide as an ambassador for the Royal family. This fact perhaps undermines Meghan's assertion that she was silenced and no longer allowed a platform for her voice. However, Meghan was advised not to stand up for herself against defamatory tabloid news. All newcomers to the family and even existing royals have endured negative press coverage. However, silence and discreet behaviour perhaps starves the press of the necessary fuel to continue with unpleasant news stories. Unfortunately, Harry's behaviour seems to have spurred the Press on. Harry stated *"I fully accept that writing a book is feeding the beast."*[66]

Meghan has received more negative press than the Princess of Wales. Yet, according to research, between May 2018 and January 2020, 56% of tabloid articles about Meghan were either

---

[65] (Royal.UK, 2019)

[66] (GMA, 2023)

positive or neutral in tone. This figure only accounts for coverage in 14 print newspapers.[67] A recent poll shows the popularity of both Harry and Meghan has plummeted since the release of their expose into the Royal family. *"Almost two-thirds (64%) of Britons have a negative view of Harry, up from 58% in May, with just a quarter (26%) seeing him in a positive light, according to the YouGov survey. Harry's net favourability among the British public is at an all-time low of minus 38, with his wife, the Duchess of Sussex, recording minus 42."*[68]

Their strategy to fight the Press and the monarchy may not be the best course of action. Saturating the media with positive PR regarding their good work and their charitable endeavours, could potentially drown out the naysayers. However, when Meghan received glowing press coverage of her tour of Australia, Tonga, Fiji and New Zealand,

---

[67] (Duncan, 2020)
[68] (GMA, 2023)

and a standing ovation for her speech, Harry stated *"you're doing too well my love. Too damn well. You're making it look too easy."* He made comparisons with his mother, stating the situation could go from *"bad to worse [if she] showed the world, showed the family that she was better at connecting with people, better at being 'royal' than she had any right to be"* (p.350). Harry actively dissuaded his wife from 'doing a great job,' being successful and generating "exultant headlines." Therefore, it was Meghan's husband, Harry, who was in fact suppressing and silencing Meghan because of his own distorted perception of danger and fear of 'history repeating itself (and possibly resenting her stealing the limelight). Perhaps this was the time Meghan began to be affected vicariously by her husband's fears. She stated she noticed a change after the Australia tour.

She stated *"I knew we weren't being protected. And it was during that part of my pregnancy, especially, that I started to understand what our continued reality was going to look like."*[69]

By Royal standards, Harry and Meghan had a whirlwind romance and impetuous marriage. More so, given that they had a long-distance relationship. Harry stated *"I've always told myself that there were firm rules about relationships, at least when it came to royalty, and the main one was that you absolutely must date a woman for three years before taking the plunge. How else could she know about you and your royal life?"* (p.284). Harry ignored his own rule, his own counsel and became engaged to Meghan after only fifteen months of courtship. Harry longed for a wife and children – not least to feel accepted and valued within his own family and to feel of worth (p.231, p.238). He saw all the attributes he needed in Meghan as his partner for life. Independent,

---

[69] (Markle M. , 2021)

ambitious, capable, intelligent, adventurous, successful in her own right, capable of withstanding the spotlight and media attention. Meghan's character and lifestyle were compatible with his desire to be free.

Prince Harry never met Meghan's father Mr Markle. Her half-sister, Samantha Markle is taking Meghan to court over allegations of defamation.[70] The only family member Meghan invited to her wedding was her mother. It seems Meghan isolated herself from her family and isolated Harry from his. Or perhaps Harry was the person who isolated them both. This is a worrying sign and often a red flag in cases of coercion and control in relationships. However, they do appear to enjoy friendships with others. Harry stated Meghan had given up and sacrificed everything she knew to live in his world. Now he has done the same to live in hers.[71]

---

[70] (Donlevy, 2023)
[71] (Sussex, 2022)

Harry went into the relationship with unresolved, intense shame at being publicly humiliated and accused of racism (p.103-105, 249). Harry stated, *"I cared about people not thinking I was a racist. I cared about not being a racist"* (p.162).

"I got called a racist when I was in my 20s by mistakes that I made. They were never intentional to harm anybody, but I recognise a level of unconscious bias within me that probably came from a combination of my upbringing, things I was exposed to and things that I saw in the media. And I made a choice to right that wrong. I wanted to be part of the solution rather than part of the problem. And that has taken a lot of hard work, because I couldn't understand 'why am I being called a racist?' of course clearly by what I did it looked that way. But I knew that I wasn't a racist.

I made an active choice to ensure that the British press and the public knew that I wasn't because that was a horrible place to be, a horrible thing to be called."[72]

Harry has criticised the Royal family for not supporting his wife by making public statements to condemn the "wave of abuse and harassment" in the tabloid press, including an underlying tone of racism. Harry, through Kensington Palace released a statement on the 8th November 2016 to this end, only a few months after Harry and Meghan's relationship had been confirmed. This statement did not result in the cessation of Meghan's negative press. Therefore, Harry's comment that the monarchy's silence is a betrayal, [73] is perhaps an unfair criticism. The monarchy's public relations experts warned that Harry would only be fuelling the Press if he responded. However, Harry felt silence was not an option (p.300). He *"felt wild with rage and*

---

[72] (Mohan-Hickson, 2023)
[73] (Cooper, 2023)

guilt." Harry read an article, which stated *"the mild reaction of Britons to this explosion of racism [regarding Meghan] was to be expected, since they were the heirs of racist colonialists. But what was truly unforgivable [is Harry's] silence"* (p.300). Therefore, Harry was branded a racist colonialist. It was in fact Harry's own perceived betrayal, which needed to be rectified. Any accusation that Harry is racist, reignites his feelings of intense humiliation and shame and this leads to feelings of rage. Shame can create narcissism and may elicit rumination on a plan for revenge against the person who triggered the shame. Harry certainly seems embittered and angry toward the Press.[74]

Meghan had a different approach to the media. She was interviewed by Vanity Fair in October 2017, nearly one year since the Kensington Palace statement was made. The article stated *"The media frenzy seems to bother the prince more than it does Markle. The official statement issued from*

---

[74] (Carter, 2021)

Kensington Palace by his communications secretary read, in part, "Meghan Markle has been subject to a wave of abuse and harassment...Prince Harry is worried about Ms Markle's safety and is deeply disappointed that he has not been able to protect her.' As for Markle, she prefers what the British call 'ostriching.' She says, "I don't read any press. I haven't even read press for Suits [the TV show Meghan featured in]. The people who are close to me anchor me in knowing who I am. The rest is noise."[75] Harry's account in 'Spare' (2023) correlates with Meghan's interview (2017). He stated *"As a rule, Meg wasn't looking at the internet. She wanted to protect herself, keep that poison out of her brain. Smart, but not sustainable if we were going to wage a battle for her reputation and physical safety. I needed to know exactly what was fact, what was false, and that meant asking her every few hours about something else that had appeared online. She'd often begin to cry"* (p.301).

---

[75] (Kashner, 2017)

This is perhaps further supporting evidence of Harry's posttraumatic symptoms and blame, as well as the potential for Meghan to suffer from vicarious trauma. She clearly had a successful coping strategy, to avoid reading Press stories. The same strategy used by other senior Royals. In essence, everyone agreed it was best to ignore the tabloid articles, except for Harry who forced Meghan to digest the offensive material, subjecting her to distress and his perception of danger.

When Harry and Meghan formally announced their engagement to the Press, Harry deliberately held a press conference from a distance. Meghan was never introduced to the Press properly. Though Meghan was happy to build a relationship with the media, Harry deterred her from doing so, warning her that she didn't understand what could happen if she did. This was viewed as a mistake according to the Royal correspondent for the Daily Express.[76] As Meghan became more isolated from her old life, she became more susceptible to Harry's perception of danger.

Perhaps Harry's genuine love for Meghan, who is biracial, would help Harry to heal from his past injuries and show the world he does not have racism in his heart. Harry stated Meghan would have been an asset to the monarchy, particularly in light of the racial demographic of the Commonwealth. He stated, there was a missed opportunity by the Royal family.[77] Does Harry suggest his choice of wife was a strategic move to promote himself in a positive light and to modernise the monarchy?

Meghan's values of freedom, independence, ambition and unfettered opinion would be unlikely to fit the job specification for a working, high profile Royal. This is perhaps the equivalent of awarding someone with a promotion to a

---

[76] (Rajan, 2021)

[77] (GMA, 2023)

senior role based on ethnicity or race, and not ability – not recruiting someone because they are right for the role and employing them for a positive public image. Is Harry somehow objectifying Meghan? Harry stated "*With the family, particularly the men, there can be temptation or urge to marry someone who would fit the mould, rather than someone you're destined to be with.*"[78]

During a TV interview the host stated "*you accused members of your family of racism.* Harry replied, "*No I didn't. The British press said that. Did Meghan ever mention that they're racist?* The host stated "*she said there were troubling comments about Archie's skin colour. There was concern about his skin colour. Wouldn't you describe that as essentially racist?* Harry replied "*the difference between racism and unconscious bias, the two things are different. unconscious bias then moves into the category of racism.*[79] Harry seems to be

---

78 (Sussex, 2022)
79 (Mohan-Hickson, 2023)

'playing with words' and trying to retract Meghan's implication that the Royal family are racist. When Harry later joined the interview in question with his wife, he discovered Meghan had exposed the comment about their baby's skin colour without his agreement. He seemed uncomfortable that she had done so, perhaps knowing how it feels to be accused of racism. He refused to comment on the incident further. This may suggest Meghan predicted the reaction of the Press (after putting the cat amongst the pigeons), giving the media just enough information to create a furore and an opportunity to positively promote her and her husband as champions of racial justice, for which Harry and Meghan received an award.[80]

Despite their denial, the comments made during the interview were significant enough to provoke a rebuttal from Queen Elizabeth II on the 9th March 2021, stating *"The issues raised,*

---

[80] (Bedigan, 2022)

particularly that of race, are concerning. Whilst some recollections may vary, they are taken very seriously."[81] Furthermore, Harry stated in 'Spare,' that *"there were whispers about a vague and pervasive unease regarding [Meghan's] race. Concern had been expressed in certain corners about whether or not Britain was ready"* (p.322), not whether the Royal family was ready. Interestingly, Meghan had not been privy to the alleged racist remarks. Harry chose to tell his pregnant wife something that would undoubtedly cause her distress.

Queen Elizabeth II had given her blessing for the marriage; Harry's father had stated he adored Meghan. Harry stated, "it *filled my heart to see my father treating [Meghan] like the princess she was about to become"* (p.330).

At no point did Prince William tell Harry not to marry the woman he loves. Harry stated William liked Meghan and did not hesitate in agreeing to

---

[81] (BBC, 2021)

Harry "*harvesting the diamonds from one particularly beautiful bracelet [belonging to their mother, Princess Diana], to fashion an engagement ring for Meghan.*" Harry noted the Duchess of Cambridge liked Meghan too (p.324). Harry describes how members of his family adored Meghan, and made her feel welcomed and valued.

However, Harry stated 'silence is betrayal' and allows injustice to continue. This comment was made regarding the abuse of his wife by the Press and his family's refusal to make a public statement supporting her. Yet, it appears he did not make a statement in support of Lady Susan Hussey when she was accused of racism in the media at the time of the incident, which resulted in her resignation after decades of service to Queen Elizabeth II. He remained silent, until a TV interview to promote his memoir where he stated both he and his wife, Meghan, held Lady Hussey in high regard. By then it was too late. He stated "*Meghan and I, love Susan Hussey. She thinks she's great. And I also know that what she meant – she never meant any harm at all. But the response from the British Press, and from people online because of the stories that they wrote was horrendous. Was absolutely horrendous."*[82]

The evidence suggests Meghan was treated well by Royalty and she was accepted as a member of the family. That said, one might venture that Harry somewhat blindsided Meghan and rushed her to the altar before she had a chance to experience the 'reality' of life as a Royal – and an opportunity to withdraw. Harry's previous partners, who had also been adventurous, free-spirited and independent, would not sacrifice their intrinsic values, such as freedom, in exchange for the trappings of royal life and the scrutiny of the Press.

Harry believes Meghan knew little to nothing of his family or what to expect as a royal. Meghan

---

[82] (Mohan-Hickson, 2023)

did not research the monarchy.[83] Her lack of prior interest in the Royal family was another attractive quality for Harry (p.94). Meghan stated, she relied on Harry to tell her all she needed to know. Perhaps Harry felt the less she knew, the less chance of losing her. Was Meghan's lack of interest deliberate to captivate Harry? or did Harry control Meghan by withholding important information from her? Or is this an example of two people in love hoping none of this mattered?

The host of one interview with the Duchess challenged her on this issue. She asked *"Everybody who gets married knows you're really marrying the family. But you weren't just marrying a family, you were marrying a 1,200-year-old institution, you're marrying the monarchy. What did you think it was going to be like?"*

Meghan replied, *"I would say I went into it naively because I didn't grow up knowing much about the*

---

[83] (Markle M. , 2021)

Royal Family. It wasn't part of something that was part of conversation at home. It wasn't something that we followed. My mum even said to me a couple of months ago, 'Did Diana ever do an interview?' Now I can say. 'Yes, a very famous one', but my mum doesn't know that." The host challenged her again. *"But you were aware of the royals and, if you were going to marry into the royals, you'd do research about what that would mean?"* Meghan insisted, *"I didn't do any research about what that would mean. I didn't feel any need to, because everything I needed to know he was sharing with me. Everything we thought I needed to know, he was telling me."* The interviewer was unconvinced. *"So, you didn't have a conversation with yourself, or talk to your friends about what it would be like to marry a prince, who is Harry, who you had fallen in love with. You didn't give it a lot of thought?"* Meghan stated, *"No. We thought a lot about what we thought it might be. I didn't fully understand what the job was: What does it mean to be a working royal? What do you do? What does that mean? He and I were very aligned on our cause-driven work, that was part of our initial connection. But there was no way to understand what the day-to- day was going to be like, and it's so different because I didn't romanticise any element of it. But I think, as Americans especially, what you do know about the royals is what you read in fairy tales, and you think it is what you know about the royals. It's easy to have an image that is so far from reality, and that's what was so tricky over those past few years, when the perception and the reality are two different things and you're being judged on the perception but you're living the reality of it. There's a complete misalignment and there's no way to explain that to people."[84]*

Although it seems incredulous that Meghan had not researched the Royal family, Harry stated his previous partner (Chelsy) was also uninterested in his title and was bored by it. She was not in the least bit curious and was not affected by 'throne

---

[84] (Markle M. , 2021)

syndrome.' Harry stated *"I'd always wanted to know what it might be like to meet a woman and not have her eyes widen at the mention of my title, but instead to widen them myself, using my mind, my heart"* (p.94). Perhaps it is unfair to assume Meghan was calculating when she claimed not to have any curiosity about the Royal family when entering a relationship with Harry.

We may never know if Meghan was acutely aware of Prince Harry's preference for a woman with no designs on him for his wealth and royal status, and whether she deliberately mimicked Chelsy. However, as a socialite, seeking a network with high profile celebrities, it is difficult to imagine Harry's position was of no interest to her. Unfortunately, Meghan's claim of ignorance of royal life comes unstuck when it is disclosed that she was friends with Princess Eugenie (Queen Elizabeth's granddaughter) prior to her meeting Harry. Furthermore, Harry stated Meghan did not recognise Prince Andrew (Eugenie's father), at a family gathering. Harry took this as further evidence Meghan had not researched the family and therefore, was only interested in him and not his status or connections (p.293).[85]

During an interview, Meghan stated *"Eugenie and I had known each other before I knew Harry."* She stated it was comfortable having Eugenie's mother present when meeting Queen Elizabeth II for the first time. She stated, *"Fergie ran out and said, 'Are you ready? Do you know how to curtsey?"*

In addition to these revelations, Harry and Eugenie have always been close. These facts seem to cast doubt on Meghan's claim she did not know what to expect from entering the Royal household or the traits Harry would find attractive.

People may remember when Fergie and Princess Diana supported each other with a rebellion against life as a Royal, before Fergie self-exiled to America after her divorce. Both Fergie and Diana struggled with the consequences of being part of

---

[85] (Markle M. , 2021)

the monarchy and found a kindred spirit in each other. Diana and Fergie were tumultuous friends and allies. They were also cousins.[86] With this in mind, it is difficult to believe Meghan had no knowledge of the potential pitfalls and how her life would change before entering into an engagement with Harry. Eugenie and Fergie have both experienced the ravages of the tabloid press. Did they not warn Meghan in any way? And are we to believe, she did not research the Royal family, as she claims?[87]

Furthermore, Meghan stated *"three days before our wedding, we got married."*[88] Meghan implies the Royal wedding witnessed by the nation and the world, was not the legal ceremony. However, this statement has been blasted by the Archbishop of Canterbury as incorrect - stating this would be illegal. [89] These examples of

---

[86] (Moody, 2022)
[87] (Markle M. , 2021)
[88] (Markle M. , 2021)
[89] (PA-Reporters, 2021)

potential misinformation and mistruths may cast doubt on Meghan's version of events and the reliability of her words.

Those closest to Meghan describe her as compassionate, empathetic, warm, fun, congenial, mature, easy to get along with and sociable. Meghan has the same awkward photos and home videos most of us have during childhood and adolescence. She described herself as a nerd – smart, not beautiful and a good student growing up. Meghan stated she was a daddy's girl and with him a lot, but lonely and wanted more people around her. Others are cynical and suspicious of her nature and her motives. What is perhaps reasonable to assume, is that, like anyone else, her character changed under extreme levels of stress, fear, trepidation, and being forced to supress her personality. Perhaps if Harry had not prohibited Meghan from interacting with the Press, people could have had the opportunity to know her at her best.

Harry and Meghan seem to unfairly criticise the monarchy. The senior Royals are bound by strict protocols, rules and the need to maintain their way of life. For what reigning monarch could tolerate the collapse of an historic institution dating back over one thousand years 'on their watch?' Even Queen Elizabeth II did not have the power to help her grandson and his wife, in the ways Harry and Meghan wanted.

Harry *"suggested that the late Queen's hands were tied when it came to helping him and his wife. "She knew what was going on. She knew how hard it was. I don't know whether she was in a position to be able to change it."* [90] Therefore, it seems unreasonable for Harry and Meghan to blame King Charles III for the abuse Meghan suffered at the hands of the Press, or to hold him accountable.

Though the monarchy accepted Harry's decision to emigrate and to abdicate from his role as a senior working Royal; wishing him well. Harry

---

[90] (GMA, 2023)

seems 'hell-bent' on beating the monarchy into submission – until they bend to his will - to acquiesce to him. He demands they take accountability for all the injustices Harry perceives.[91] His querulous nature is suggestive of MI and PB (including persistent embitterment and distorted perceptions).

During an interview, Harry was asked if there was any possibility of him and Meghan returning to Britain as working royals, to which he replied "I *don't think it's ever going to be possible.* "[92] Was it always his intention to make it impossible to return? Harry stated, *"I feel safe here [in California], my family feel safe here, I'm happy, my family's happy, it's difficult going back."* [93] Harry stated, flying back into London is a trigger to his symptoms of anxiety and he has to draw on the 'tools in his toolbox' to cope with the

[91] (Mohan-Hickson, 2023)
[92] (GMA, 2023)
[93] (Mohan-Hickson, 2023)

experience.[94] Harry stated, *"You know the things that trigger you, so you stay away from that."*[95]

His insistence on an apology from the Royal family in exchange for his attendance at the King's coronation, is perhaps an example of Harry's avoidance. He knows an apology is unlikely to be forthcoming and this gives him the excuse he needs to 'stay away from' the factors which, exacerbate his posttraumatic symptoms. Yet, Harry and Meghan know they need to remain relevant and in the public eye to generate an income.

Harry appears ambivalent about accountability to the public when he was a senior Royal, and subsequent Press interest in his affairs. In an interview, Harry was asked *"I just want to be clear, are you really saying that, third in line to the throne or whatever you were, you taking a class A drug is not a matter of public interest? Cause I think that's*

---

[94] (ET-Canada, 2021)
[95] (Today, 2022)

a question people will have. Do you accept that is a matter of public interest for the press?" Harry stated "*the relationship between the institution [the monarchy] and the tabloid media should be of greater interest to the public.*"[96]

Harry admits he deftly denied habitual use of illicit drugs as escapism from his emotional distress in the past. Harry accused the Press of lying when challenged about Cocaine. He stated, "(the journalist) *is a liar. It's not true.*" However, he then stated, *"Of course, I had been doing cocaine around this time at someone's country house, during a shooting weekend (p.76). I was ashamed for lying. But also proud. In a tight spot, a hugely scary crisis,*" Harry claims he was able to project serenity, which masked his lies (p.77). Prolific lying to hide addictions and associated guilt and shame, is not uncommon. However, this disclosure may cast doubt over his honesty and trustworthiness.

---

[96] (Mohan-Hickson, 2023)

Harry states "*I don't understand how so much of what has happened from one version, one side of this story, how me telling the other side, the truthful side, is so shocking and outrageous*"[97] Yet, what emerges from Spare and recent interviews to promote the release of Harry's memoir, is that the statements, interpretations, perceptions, beliefs and recollections of the Duke and Duchess of Sussex cannot be relied upon as fact and may be distorted cognitions. Research findings lead one to conclude that disclosures made by Harry and Meghan could be unreliable.

Harry stated in his interview that Meghan was always going to leave because of the way she felt treated badly by the Royal family and she exhibited distress and suicidal thoughts during pregnancy (p.354). Harry was forced to make a decision to leave the UK and step away from Royal duties with his wife, when their son was nine months old. Harry may have been faced with the

---

[97] (Wood, 2023)

prospect of being separated from his child, should he remain with the Royal family and in the UK.

It is not clear if Meghan's pregnancy contributed to her feelings of hopelessness, desperation and suicidal ideation. Perhaps Meghan was feeling trapped, stifled and silenced in a way which was untenable for her and somewhat unexpected. Perhaps Meghan wanted to isolate Harry from his family and threatened suicide during pregnancy to this end. Perhaps they were both genuinely struggling and knew the only way they could both feel better, was to leave.

Meghan's feelings of mistreatment seem to stem from a difficult transition into the tradition and culture of the monarchy. Yet Harry stated his father, King Charles III had bonded with her (p.315). Anna Pasternak, author of 'Princess in Love,' stated, Meghan had an agenda that once she was a member of the Royal family, she would have a platform for her voice, which was never going to be possible. She apparently rubbed people up the wrong way very quickly. Harry and Meghan wanted to change the way 'things were done' within the Royal family and expeditiously so.[98]

Harry stated Meghan's life plan was to *"help people, do some good and be free"* (p.273). Meghan was an actor, a *"lifestyle writer, travel writer, corporate spokesperson, entrepreneur, activist, model and worked for the US embassy in Argentina"* for a time (p.272). Therefore, it seems Meghan was used to going after what she wanted and having the freedom to vocalise her opinions. This is in contrast to the Royal family, who must remain apolitical. King Charles III himself, has been criticised in the past for being vocal about issues of importance to him, such as climate change (p.315).

Meghan does not seem to have a main focus or one main effort in relation to vocation or employment. Rather it seems she has a scattergun approach, casting her net wide in search of ways

---

[98] (Rajan, The Princes and the Press, 2021)

to raise her profile, connect with high profile individuals and climb the social ladder. Was becoming royalty her main ambition?

Harry and Meghan had a long-distance courtship, which is not the same as living normal day to day life together. It seems Meghan's expectations of life as a Royal were not the reality.

The Duke and Duchess wished to reform an ancient monarchy in their own image, which caused rifts in Royal relationships and possibly led to a conflagration. [99] Harry and Meghan decided to leave the Royal family and the UK fearing for their psychological health, if not their physical safety.

Harry loosely draws comparison with the abdicated King Edward VIII and his decision to leave the monarchy to be with the woman he loved - an American divorcee (p.2). However, the monarchy supported Harry's marriage to an

---

[99] (Rajan, 2021)

American biracial, divorced actor (p.329), which is a significant and progressive concession.

Furthermore, King Edward's departing words in his address to the nation on 12th December 1936 are in stark contrast to Harry's bitter memoir.

King Edward VIII: 12th December 1936

At long last I am able to say a few words of my own. I have never wanted to withhold anything, but until now it has not been constitutionally possible for me to speak.

A few hours ago I discharged my last duty as King and Emperor, and now that I have been succeeded by my brother, the Duke of York, my first words must be to declare my allegiance to him. This I do with all my heart.

You all know the reasons which have impelled me to renounce the throne. But I want you to understand that in making up my mind I did not forget the country or the empire, which, as Prince of Wales, and lately as King, I have for 25 years tried to serve.

But you must believe me when I tell you that I have found it impossible to carry the heavy burden of responsibility and to discharge my duties as King as I would wish to do without the help and support of the woman I love.

And I want you to know that the decision I have made has been mine and mine alone. This was a thing I had to judge entirely for myself. The other person most nearly concerned has tried up to the last to persuade me to take a different course.

I have made this, the most serious decision of my life, only upon the single thought of what would, in the end, be best for all.

This decision has been made less difficult to me by the sure knowledge that my brother, with his long training in the public affairs of this country and with his fine qualities, will be able to take my place forthwith without interruption or injury to the life and progress of the empire. And he has one matchless blessing, enjoyed by so many of you, and not bestowed on me -- a happy home with his wife and children.

During these hard days I have been comforted by her majesty my mother and by my family. The ministers of the crown, and in particular, Mr. Baldwin, the Prime Minister, have always treated me with full consideration. There has never been any constitutional difference between me and them, and between me and Parliament. Bred in the constitutional tradition by my father, I should never have allowed any such issue to arise.

Ever since I was Prince of Wales, and later on when I occupied the throne, I have been treated with the greatest kindness by all classes of the people wherever I have lived or journeyed throughout the empire. For that I am very grateful.

I now quit altogether public affairs and I lay down my burden. It may be some time before I return to my native land, but I shall always follow the fortunes of the British race and empire with profound interest, and if at any time in the future I can be found of service to his majesty in a private station, I shall not fail.

And now, we all have a new King. I wish him and you, his people, happiness and prosperity with all my heart. God bless you all. God save the King![100]

The abdicated King spoke with generosity, humility, loyalty, allegiance, dignity and implored the nation to empathise with his desire to be with the woman he loved. Reading King Edward's speech perhaps affords King Charles III and Camilla, the Queen Consort, respect and admiration for their own resilience and endurance in their struggle as star-crossed lovers, who fell deeply in love and could not be together due to external circumstances, now happily remedied by their union on 9th April 2005. "*Full acceptance from Queen Elizabeth II took time, but in her final years she was unequivocal in her*

---

[100] (Windsor, 2017)

support for Camilla."[101] When viewed in this light, Harry is most fortunate to have had the blessing of his family to marry the woman of his choosing, to step away from royal duties, to emigrate to foreign lands and to have his desired freedom and independence – no longer required to sacrifice his own desires for the sake of service to the British nation or the Commonwealth.

Furthermore, The King may have agreed to the departure of the Duke and Duchess of Sussex from royal duties due to the cost of supporting them and their children. Apparently, he had told Harry there is not enough money to go around. Harry stated *"Pa didn't financially support [us] out of any largesse. That was his job. That was the whole deal. We agreed to serve the monarch, go wherever we were sent, do whatever we were told, surrender our autonomy, keep our hands and feet inside the gilded cage at all times, and in exchange the keepers of the cage agreed to feed and clothe us,"*

---

[101] (Campbell, 2022)

(p.320) and provide personal security and support staff and fund travel and any other costs incurred.

Harry stated the Royal family are fearful of public opinion and that one day the nation would demand the dissolution of the monarchy, as they are too costly (p.237).

If the Royal family continue the recent trend of marrying 'commoners,' (such as Kate Middleton and Meghan Markle) could the public begin to question what it means to be royalty? If the aristocracy continues to become diluted with 'ordinary folk', these could become questions for the future. Will the public wish to fund a family of 'celebrities?' Perhaps this will depend upon the ability of newcomers to assimilate into the culture of the monarchy and prove themselves as exceptional role models with a higher degree of morality than the British mob, such as Kate Middleton who executes her role as a senior Royal with aplomb.

People will gladly support their leaders and afford them all the 'perks' they feel that person has earned. This means their leaders must not breach the 'contract' of such privilege. The public expect their leaders to act in the best interests of their followers, even if the leader must suffer or make sacrifices to do so. [102] Harry implies the public get value for money as justification for his sense of entitlement to public funds. He stated *"the monarchy costs the average tax payer, the cost of a pint"* (p.386).

Harry perhaps fails to understand that the issue of cost relates to the public view of whether Royalty are deserving of an opulent lifestyle, when they are themselves struggling.

King Charles III, stated *"Being born as a Windsor is a privilege, but it doesn't mean that being a certain number in line to the throne means an entitlement to housing and other perks of The Firm. He went on to say that stripping back the royals may also be*

---

[102] (Sinek, 2017)

beneficial to those who aren't keen to live a life in the public eye. 'Prince Charles and Prince William have no choice in the matter, and nor will Prince George in due course,' he pointed out. But he added that for some, being a royal is both a 'gift and personal choice."[103] Taken in light of the King's words and what is known of his compassion for his children, it is with regret that Harry did not simply decide to leave the monarchy on good terms. He could have announced to the world that he felt he was needed elsewhere and left to focus on other activities. With the millions of pounds left to him by his mother, Harry had the networks and financial security he needed to be independent of the monarchy for life. Had he asked his father for support with his decision, he most likely would have given it. So, the question is why didn't Harry make this move? Harry stated he hadn't been a full-time working Royal by the time he left the military and he wasn't sure it was something he wanted to do. So, it wasn't as if he

---

[103] (Morgan, 2020)

didn't know how to be anything other than a senior royal. Harry stated he felt trapped. The evidence suggests, he wasn't trapped by the monarchy. He was trapped by his own dependency on royal status, royal protection, public funds, negative self-concept, perceived lack of intelligence, talent or skill and addiction to the Press attention.

What becomes apparent after considering the evidence thus far, is that Harry's decisions and choices are responsible for the unfortunate manner in which he left the monarchy, the animosity he has for his family and the impact on Meghan. Harry stated *"Anybody else in my situation would have done exactly the same thing."* However, this simply is not the case, which is why the Duke and Duchess of Sussex have become unpopular with the public in the UK and other parts of the world.

Prince Harry – A case study for Moral Injury and Posttraumatic Blame

"I felt wild with rage….the anger came from somewhere deep inside that needed to be excavated" (Duke of Sussex)

Harry's memoir 'Spare' is largely anecdotal and uneventful and describes family relationships, that are not uncommon - familial love and affection, clashes in personality, solidarity, disagreement, sibling rivalry and estrangement. Harry's desire to achieve, have meaning and purpose in life and the juxtaposition of ambition with a desire to go unnoticed - living a normal life, are perhaps a sign of the times, where celebrity is a sign of success and sometimes attracts unpleasant attention.

Overall, three significant themes emerge in the book 'Spare', which can be triangulated. 1) His mother's violent, unexpected and traumatic death when he was 12 years of age, leading to 2) distorted perceptions regarding her death. His attribution of blame towards the British tabloid Press and developing a potentially pathological embitterment towards the media and 3) Harry believes he lacks talent and academic ability. He appears to resent his position of birth as spare to the heir. Furthermore, Harry has been plagued by the speculation of others over his legitimacy. These factors seem to lead to a dependency on the British press for a sense of identity. For example, a victim's dependency on their abuser for survival. In other words, his claim to fame is his mother, royal status and his role as a celebrity 'being the naughty one.' He states "*I had no talent—so I'd been told, again and again—and thus all reactions to me had nothing to do with me. They were down to my family, my title, and consequently they always embarrassed me, because they were so unearned*" (p.94).

Harry perhaps feels the need to keep the embittered feud with the press alive – to ruminate on his persistent perception that the Press is a danger to him and his family. He speaks of having to flee his own country for safety. However, he appears addicted to press attention and provoking the danger he perceives.

After his mother's death, Harry remembers reaching for his father's hand as a child, seeking reassurance and comfort, which *"set off an explosion of [camera] clicks."* He stated *"I'd given them exactly what they wanted. Emotion, Drama. Pain"* (p.20). Harry is still feeding the Press now. One might wonder if this incident created a lasting cognition that showing emotion is bad and may have reinforced emotional numbing, resentment, bitterness and anger.

Harry felt ashamed for *"violating the family ethos"* when he sobbed uncontrollably after his mother's coffin was lowered into the ground. Yet, he felt able to reassure himself that this emotional outburst was okay because there were no cameras around to capture the moment, only close family members (p.25).

Harry's dependency on the Press was made clear when he stated he was obsessively searching for stories about his wife in the media and described this as an addiction.[104] Harry stated *"my father had begged me to stop thinking about the press, to not reading the papers. I admitted that I felt guilty every time I did, because it made me complicit"* (p.219).

Perhaps Harry was unconsciously seeking ammunition and further grudge against the Press, which affords him both pain and pleasure – an identified symptom of rumination, and therefore MI and PB.[105] Harry stated he has now weaned himself off this activity and is on 'a digital diet' to protect his mental health. [106] Perhaps this behaviour demonstrates recklessness or danger seeking associated with posttraumatic stress. Or that Harry would be no-one of consequence without press coverage and his status as one of

---

[104] (Colbert, 2023)
[105] (Linden & Maercker, 2011)
[106] (Colbert, 2023)

Princess Diana's sons. Harry stated *"when it came to the press, [Pa] hated their hate, but oh how he loved their love"* (p.396), which seems to be a projection of his own 'painful and pleasurable' relationship with the Press. Camilla Tominey (journalist), in the BBC documentary the Princes and the Press (2021) stated, Harry was becoming increasingly popular with the public and so the Press were mindful not to be critical of him. He has a 'love-hate' relationship with the press.[107]

Harry stated *"the press had been cruel to me. Sometimes I'd asked for it, brought it on myself."* (p.358). For example, Harry stated he deserved the backlash from the Press for wearing a Nazi uniform to a fancy-dress party, which brought him intense feelings of shame (p.103). His father empathized with Harry's humiliation. Harry spoke with the chief Rabbi of Britain. He felt *"bottomless self-loathing"* and appreciated the Rabbi's teachings on forgiveness of oneself

---

[107] (Rajan, The Princes and the Press, 2021)

(p.106). Yet Harry appears to have difficulty with forgiveness. He stated *"I might learn to endure the press, and even forgive their abuse, I might, but my own family's complicity—that was going to take longer to get over* (p.455). Forgiveness, may feel like rewarding the perpetrator for the harmful or bad behaviour. Perhaps more so, where the perpetrator of the injury has not been held accountable. Harry stated *"There's a lot that I can forgive, but there needs to be conversations in order for reconciliation, and part of that has to be accountability."*[108]

One may find the thought of forgiveness wholly abhorrent and may become angry at the suggestion.[109] Pressure may come to bear, from friends, family or religious communities. This may cause significant stress or frustration, if one feels unable to forgive. One may feel duty bound not to forgive - equating forgiveness as forgetting, particularly when loved ones have been

[108] (GMA, 2023)
[109] (Linden & Maercker, 2011)

victimised, injured or lost. Perhaps one feels that to forgive what happened is to lose a sense of meaning and purpose derived from the experience. [110] Harry stated the pain he feels relating to the loss of his mother is all that keeps him moving and "the only thing holding [him] together" (p.309). So, why would Harry want to forgive his family or the Press, if this would result in him giving up on life? What kind of empty void would there be without the pain? How mundane and boring would life be, without that addiction? Difficulty with forgiveness is synonymous with MI and PB.

Harry stated in an interview, *"I think there's probably a lot of people who, after watching the documentary and reading the book, will go, how could you ever forgive your family for what they've done? People have already said that to me. And I said, forgiveness is 100% a possibility because I would like to get my father back. I would like to*

---

[110] (Carter, 2020)

have my brother back. At the moment, I don't recognize them, as much as they probably don't recognize me."[111] Harry has blinkered himself to the perception that the public empathize with the way he feels treated by his family. Though arguably there is significantly greater public admonishment of his behaviour.

Harry refers to a negative self-concept and "nonstop internal self-criticism" throughout his life (p.83). He "berated" himself for trusting others, calling himself "stupid" for doing so.

After turning to drugs and alcohol in his youth, stories were leaked to the Press. He asked himself "How had I let [this] happen?" (p.242). It seems Harry felt betrayed by those around him and lost trust in himself and others. Both of these feelings are indicative of MI and PB. Harry's self-esteem was rock-bottom. He stated, "the *fact was, I didn't believe in myself, didn't believe in much of*

---

[111] (Mohan-Hickson, 2023)

anything, least of all me. Sometimes the self-loathing would spill onto" [others] (p.169). He stated he didn't know how to be proud of himself, until he had succeeded in the military.

Harry writes about his feelings of enduring guilt that he was unable to express emotion at the death of his mother, particularly when the public who thought they knew her (but didn't), were grieving. He worried his mother would think he did not love her because he did not cry.[112] Yet, Harry stated he believed his mother was not really dead and was in hiding somewhere, waiting for the right time to reunite with her sons. He believed this between twelve years and twenty-three years of age – eleven years of distorted cognitions. It is unsurprising that Harry could not grieve if he believed his mother was still alive.[113]

Harry continued to suffer with feelings of low self-worth when trying to protect his wife from the

---

[112] (Mohan-Hickson, 2023)
[113] (Cooper, 2023)

danger he perceived from the Press. Harry *"felt...guilt. [he had] infected Meg, and her mother, with [his] contagion, otherwise known as [his] life."* Harry stated "I'd *promised her that I'd keep her safe, and I'd already dropped her into the middle of this danger"* (p.346). Self-blame and negative self-concept are associated with PTSD, MI and PB. So too is 'blame-other.' Harry attributes blame to the Royal family, the monarchy and the tabloid Press for the betrayal and injustice he feels.

Harry experienced the uncontrolled, wild, red mist of rage, which would descend upon him and stop him thinking and functioning (p.55, p.71, p.114, p.132, p.201). Disproportionate anger and outbursts of rage are symptoms of MI, PB and PTSD. Harry disclosed an incident in which he spoke with anger and disrespect to Meghan and confessed to her that the anger *"came from somewhere deep inside that needed to be excavated"* (p.306). Meghan was clear she would not tolerate Harry's aggression and suggested he get professional help and support.

This is further evidence that Harry's behaviour may have had a vicarious effect on Meghan.

Harry blames his family for refusing to release public statements supporting his wife and standing up against the abuse, which led (in part) to her feeling suicidal. Harry believes his family should take accountability for what he perceives as their failure to do 'what's right.'

Harry continued to perceive the Press as a threat, stating "*Odds were, the press would cost me another person I cared about*" (p.98). He also blames the Press for the loss of his deployment to a theatre of war. The public statement was made that the "*overwrought coverage [of journalists], their wild speculations...had "exacerbated"* the threat level" (p.145). Harry equates the Press with personal loss.

In an interview, Harry stated "*Nothing of what I've done in this book or otherwise has ever been [with] any intention to harm [my family] or hurt them. After many, many years of lies being told about me and my family, there comes a point where, again, going back to the relationship between, certain members of the family and the tabloid press, those certain members have decided to get in the bed with the devil, to rehabilitate their image. The moment that rehabilitation comes at the detriment of others, me, other members of my family, then that's where I draw the line."* The interviewer stated *"Your other criticism is that too often your interests are sacrificed to [your father's] interests, certainly when it comes to the press."* Harry stated, *"I understand the need to have that relationship with the tabloid press. I do, I understand it. I don't agree with it, but I do understand it. And there have been decisions that have happened on the other side that have been incredibly hurtful. It continues. It hasn't stopped"* [114] Yet, hypocritically, Harry is dependent on a relationship with the Press too and has demonstrated no regard for his family's feelings, public reputation or 'sacrificing them on his own PR altar.' The following chapters,

---

[114] (Mohan-Hickson, 2023)

'Traumatic incident,' 'Perception of danger,' Institutional betrayal and organisational injustice,' 'Querulous litigant,' 'Delusion of grandeur,' and 'Autobiographical memory' explore further evidence that Prince Harry is perhaps a victim and a perpetrator of MI, experiences PB, and is affected by trauma.

Traumatic incident

"The last thing Mummy saw on this earth was a flashbulb"
(Duke of Sussex)

Harry describes the difficulty he has accepting the outcome of the crash investigation into his mother's death and subsequent inquiry. Harry retraced his mother's movements through the tunnel in Paris where her car had veered into a concrete pillar. He wanted to see the place of the incident for himself. However, this only seems to have created more unanswered questions. He was surprised at how straight, short and uneventful the drive through the tunnel had been (p.131).

In discussion with an interviewer, Harry was asked, *"I mean, you really believed that maybe she had just decided to disappear for a time?"* To which Harry replied, *"For a time, and then that she would call us and that we would go and join her, yeah."* The interviewer asked, *"How long did you believe that?"* Harry stated, *"Years, many, many years. And William and I talked about it as well. He had-- he had um, similar thoughts."* An excerpt from his memoir 'Spare' was read to him. *"You write in the book, "I'd often say it to myself first thing in the morning, 'Maybe this is the day. Maybe this is the day that she's going to reappear.'"* Harry responded, *"Yeah, hope. I had huge amounts of hope."* The interviewer stated, *"Harry says he believed his mother might still be alive until he was 23 and visited Paris for the first time. "*

Harry explained why he visited the site of his mother's car crash. He stated, *"I wanted to see whether it was possible driving at the speed that Henri Paul was driving that you could lose control of a car and plough into a pillar killing almost everybody in that car. I need to take this journey. I need to ride the same route."* The interviewer stated, *"Harry writes he and his brother weren't satisfied with the results of a 2006 investigation by London's Metropolitan Police, concluding Diana's driver, Henri Paul, had been drinking and the crash was a "tragic accident."* Harry explained *"William and I considered reopening the inquest. Because there were so many gaps and so many holes in it. Which just didn't add up and didn't make sense. I don't even know if* [re-opening the case is] *an option now."*

When asked, *"Do you feel you have the answers that you need to have about what happened to your mum?"* Harry stated, *"Truth be known, no. I don't think I do. And I don't think my brother does either. I don't think the world does. Do I need any more than I already know? No. I don't think it would change much."*[115]

Harry seems to suspect a conspiracy to cover up facts. Harry wanted to push for a re-investigation, which he was advised against (p.133). The inquiry had cost £12.5 million, taken three years to complete and fourteen experienced officers to investigate. Lord John Stevens, (Metropolitan Police Commissioner at the time of the incident)

---

[115] (Cooper, 2023)

was tasked with heading the inquiry into the deaths of Princess Diana and her romantic partner, Dodi Al-Fayed at the request of Mohammed Al-Fayed (father to Dodi). He was specifically asked to investigate whether MI5 and MI6 had been responsible for the car crash, on the orders of Prince Philip and the Royal family. The investigation was called operation Paget and resulted in a report of 832 pages. The conclusion was, that the incident was a tragic accident. The cause of which, was the driver (Henri Paul) being intoxicated and on prescription drugs when he was behind the wheel, paparazzi aggressively chasing the vehicle, Diana failing to wear a seatbelt and refusing her official security. Stevens claims if official security had been there that night in Paris, that crash absolutely would not have happened. In addition, a Fiat Uno had clipped the car driven by Henri Paul prior to the crash. The driver disappeared from the scene and was interviewed after the event. Stevens stated, the Fiat Uno played no part in the car crash.

Mohamed Al-Fayed was determined in his claim that the Royal family were responsible for their deaths. 104 allegations of conspiracy to murder were made and investigated. There were concerns that Dodi may have been planning to make a marriage proposal to Diana, which (it seems) was part of the conspiracy theories. Furthermore, there was a note on file that Diana had stated she was informed by reliable sources there was a plot to get rid of her via a car accident. However, little credence was given to the note and Diana was thought to have suffered paranoia.[116] This was thought to be no more than a spooky coincidence and premonition.

Harry has not forgotten the suggestion his mother was pregnant at the time of her death (a potential motivation for a car crash). In 'Spare' he stated, when interrogated during escape and evasion training, "*A woman entered, She was wearing a shemagh over her face. She was talking about my*

---

[116] (Stern, 2022)

mother. "Your mother was pregnant when she died, eh? With your sibling? A Muslim baby!" There was a debrief, during which one of the instructors offered a half-arsed apology about the stuff to do with my mother. "Hard for us to find something about you, that you'd be shocked we knew" (p.195); the implication being that his mother's pregnancy was a fact, rather than speculation or conspiracy theory. However, the inquiry specifically addressed this concern and confirms Princess Diana was not pregnant. This interaction during escape and evasion training seems to have cast doubt, or exacerbated Harry's suspicions over the reason for his mother's death.

Harry's interviewer stated *"You made a demand of Jamie, your private secretary, that you want to see the secret government file.* Harry responded, *"I was starting to understand the involvement of the paparazzi chasing her. And to this day, I will remain eternally grateful to Jamie for showing me, what he believed I needed to see, but removing the stuff that he knew I didn't need to see. I saw the back of her blonde hair, slumped on the back of the seat. There were other photographs, that would probably show my mother's face and blood. I assume they were the ones that Jamie removed. I'm grateful to him for that. I was looking for evidence that it actually happened, that it was true. But I was also looking for something to hurt, because at that point I was still pretty numb to the whole thing."*

The interviewer went on to state *"You insist on being driven through the tunnel, at the same speed as your mother was travelling."* Harry explained, *"William and I were sat in a room, and we were told that the event was like a bicycle chain. If you remove just one of those links from the chain, the end result doesn't happen. our specific question was like, where did the paparazzi fit in that? And his response was, you remove one of those links, i.e. the paparazzi? And the result wouldn't have been the same."*

The interviewer asked *"You wanted an inquiry. Do you still have questions about that night? Is there anything about that night that you worry is still unexplained?* Harry confirmed, *"There's a lot of things that are unexplained. I've been asked before whether I want to open up another inquiry. I don't really see the point at this stage. This wonderful Irish man [drove] me through the tunnel at the same speed, there was no danger of anybody losing control even after a drink or a couple of drinks...almost physically impossible to lose control of a vehicle unless you are completely blinded at the wheel. There was multiple [times] driving back into London, I would have paparazzi literally jump on the bonnet of the car and I physically could not see anything. When you've actually experienced the same thing, which you assume your mother's driver was experiencing at the time, then it's really hard to, understand how some people have come away with the conclusions of that night.*

And that the people that were predominantly responsible for it, all got away with it.[117]

Harry stated, *"The last thing Mummy saw on this earth was a flashbulb"* (p.107). However, the fact is, Diana was treated by the paramedics on route to hospital,[118] and seven of the paparazzi were arrested at the scene. Others fled. Some paparazzi were held accountable, convicted and their sentences later quashed.[119]

The account given by the Press on scene is sickening. One can imagine the gut-wrenching disgust felt by Diana's loved ones, when faced with this reality and how this knowledge could lead to MI, PB and PTSD.

The Guardian newspaper reported *"Darmon was one of the first witnesses to arrive at the accident scene. As his photographer, Romuald Rat, got off the bike, he opened the door of the Mercedes and*

---

[117] (Mohan-Hickson, 2023)
[118] (Batty, 2007)
[119] (Balakrishnan, 2008)

said the princess was still alive. Darmon said he expected the paparazzi to help the passengers of the vehicle but was shocked when they started taking photographs. "I did not see the car anymore because the light [of the flashes] was so bright. It was continuous." Two witnesses, Antonio Lopes-Borges and Ana Simao, also testified that photographers climbed on to the car in which Diana, Dodi and Paul lay dying and took pictures instead of helping them. Such statements placed the paparazzi under suspicion for gross negligence. They were also investigated on grounds of invasion of the couple's privacy. Five days after the crash, French magistrates placed three more photographers under investigation for manslaughter, bringing the total number of suspects to 10. Nine photographers were charged with manslaughter in France but the charges were thrown out in 2002.[120]

---

[120] (Balakrishnan, 2008)

Harry stated, "I was so angry with what happened to her and the fact that there was no justice at all, nothing came from that. The same people that chased her into the tunnel photographed her dying on the back seat of that car." He began self-medicating with drugs and alcohol to deal with the pain. [121] Witnessing the photographic evidence of his mother's car crash and learning of the paparazzi's behaviour at the scene, seem to have triggered the onset of MI and PB.

---

[121] (Mountbatten-Windsor, 2021)

Perception of Danger

"I hadn't been afraid of death since the age of twelve"

(Duke of Sussex)

It is quite possible that childhood Harry suffered vicarious, inherited trauma from Princess Diana prior to her traumatic death. She stated "I *never know where a lens is going to be,*" which is a sentiment echoed by Harry. He stated he witnessed her pain and suffering. He watched her confront the Press in defence of her children's privacy. [122] Perhaps Harry is responding even now, to his mother's symptoms of trauma, as well as his own traumatic experience.

Harry describes feeling some solace and normality in the military (p.139). He served two tours in Afghanistan totalling thirty weeks during his ten years in service. His first tour lasted ten

---

[122] (Sussex, 2022)

weeks, the second tour lasted twenty weeks.[123] Harry stated his military training at Sandhurst heightened his ability to perceive threat and danger, comparing the 'click' of a photo being taken with a 'gun cocking' or a 'blade being notched open' (p.121). This exacerbated his perception of threat and danger from the Press. The sight and sounds of paparazzi did not transport him back to traumatic experiences in Afghanistan. He seems to state his training increased his pre-existing perception of the Press as a clear and present danger, (that the Press posed a substantive threat and that humiliation or harm would immediately follow). He stated, *"I remember leaving a club in London and being swarmed by twenty* [paparazzi]. *They surrounded me, then surrounded the police car in which I was sitting, threw themselves across the bonnet, all wearing football scarves around their faces and hoods over their heads, the uniform of terrorists*

---

[123] (Miller, 2021)

everywhere. It was one of the scariest moments of my life and I knew no one cared" (p.122) - Does Harry imply this experience was more frightening than being in a combat zone? If so, is his risk assessment of the Press and perception of danger distorted?

Harry has been criticised for exposing himself and his family to significant risk after disclosing his alleged kill count of 25 Taliban (p.217). Harry blamed the Press for endangering his family, by stating he had boasted about it.[124] Harry stated *"it's a lie."* He admits he made the claim, but denies 'boasting.' Harry stated *"my words are not dangerous. But the spin of my words, are very dangerous."* The interviewer asked, *"dangerous because it makes you a target, and those around you that you love?"* Harry replied the Press had made the choice to put him in danger. Harry does not take accountability for increasing the danger to himself, his family, and British citizens.

---

[124] (Colbert, 2023)

However, in 'Spare' he stated when stationed in Bastion, Afghanistan, "*the Taliban actually issued a statement: Prince Harry* [is] *our target*" (p.208). His description of removing pieces from a chess board and not thinking of the Taliban as human (p.217), has been criticised for a lack of sensitivity to the dead enemy and their families. A diplomatic faux pas as an ambassador for the Royal family and British nation, and one likely to incite terrorism. A senior Taliban leader responded to Harry's comments, stating "*Among the killers of Afghans, not many have your decency to reveal their conscience and confess war crimes.*" However, Harry stated in 'Spare' that the people he killed in Afghanistan were not on his conscience. He was neither proud nor ashamed, therefore perhaps ambivalent (p.217). Colonel Richard Kemp stated Harry has most likely given the Taliban material, which can be used for propaganda. The former head of British forces in Afghanistan was of the opinion this would heighten the risk of attack on British citizens.[125] Harry stated the backlash from his comments, which have come from within military circles was very hurtful. He was asked if the Press were deliberately trying to sabotage Harry's connection with the military, because they know how important the military community is to him. Harry stated, "of course," without doubt. His response demonstrated his distorted perception of why he had come under criticism, believing the Press coverage to be an attempt to hurt him personally, rather than recognise he had acted inappropriately. Harry appears to grab at straws and sympathy by retrospectively stating he wrote about his 'kill count' to reduce veteran suicide. He stated *"I made a choice to share it because having spent nearly two decades working with veterans all around the world – I think the most important thing is to be honest and to be able to give space to others to be able to share their experiences without*

---

[125] (ITV-News, 2023)

any shame. And my whole goal and my attempt in sharing that detail is to reduce the number of suicides."[126] Harry's argument does not stand up to scrutiny. Where is sharing your 'kill count' a recommended strategy for reducing veteran suicide? Professionals working with traumatized individuals would probably agree it is ok to discuss how a traumatic event affects behaviour, thoughts and feelings. Discussing details of an event that could traumatize others should be avoided, as this can lead to an episode of significant psychological distress. Furthermore, Harry feels no shame regarding his actions during military service.

Though Harry rebuffed the importance of his comments, he stated in his memoir that he knows *"as a soldier that turning people into non-people is the first step in mistreating them"* (p.312) and Harry has referred to Taliban fighters as chess pieces and numbers, which is dehumanising.

---

[126] (Colbert, 2023)

Therefore, he made his comments in full knowledge that they would cause offence. This incident is possibly Harry perpetrating Moral Injury.

In an interview, the host stated this was not the first time Harry had been asked about killing the enemy in Afghanistan. This happened back in 2013. Implying there had been no backlash from this in the past. The host stated, *"Another odd thing about it is that this is nothing new. Here is an article from, I believe this is from ten years ago, describing that you had killed Afghan insurgents, the Taliban, in sorties. So, this isn't new information. This has been known for a long time."*

Harry stated, he'd been asked if he killed anybody, from an attack helicopter and he said 'yes.' [127] However, in relation to his comments in 2013 Harry stated in 'Spare', that *"apparently I'd caused quite a stir by admitting that I'd killed people in a*

---

[127] (Colbert, 2023)

war. I was criticized up and down for being a killer and being blithe about it" (p.220). Therefore, Harry did not learn from this experience. Not only did he repeat history, he increased the level of offence to others with an actual 'kill count' and with his dehumanising, accompanying comments. It was not Press 'spin' that caused the increase in danger. It was Harry's own words from his own lips and it was his choice to commit those words to print.

Harry seems to have a disproportionate and distorted concept of danger - a word he frequently uses with emphasis in 'Spare.' He stated *"In a funny way I even wanted Camilla to be happy. Maybe she'd be less dangerous if she was happy?"* (p.100). Harry claims Camilla is dangerous because of her relationship with the Press.[128]

---

[128] (Cooper, 2023)

Yet, he does not perceive danger when confronting a leopard or lion up close, in the wilds of Africa (p.53, p.258), when 'taking on the Taliban,' or during flight training (p.170).

Harry stated *"I hadn't been afraid of death since the age of twelve"* (p.170). Consider Harry's level of exposure to danger since birth. His physical safety and integrity were predominantly under the protection of bodyguards and he has been placed in military roles with reduced risk to life and limb. He felt safe in his Apache helicopter (p.207). He has perhaps had less protection or personal resilience against psychological threats and attacks. This may account for the discrepancy in his seemingly warped notions of danger and where the threat is coming from. He seems more fearful of living with humiliation and shame, than dying - and all his worries and struggles dying with him.

Despite the tragedy of his mother's death, Harry's book does not describe a struggle with unusual or especially challenging adversity in life. Of course, this is a subjective view. His memoir illustrates a privileged upbringing, surrounded by people he loves and who demonstrate great affection for him, including his father and brother. Little wonder then, that his family could not understand why Harry had decided to leave the monarchy and the UK.

Harry stated, "*My childhood was filled with happiness and laughter and adventure.*" [129] Throughout 'Spare' he speaks of his family with love and affection. Yet he states, "*for* [my family] *to claim total ignorance of the reasons I'd fled the land of my birth—the land for which I'd fought and been ready to die—my Mother Country? To claim no knowledge of why my wife and I took the drastic step of picking up our child and just running like hell, leaving behind everything—house, friends,*

---

[129] (Sussex, 2022)

furniture? You don't know? Harold...I honestly don't. I turned to Pa. He was gazing at me with an expression that said: Neither do I. Wow, I thought. Maybe they really don't. Staggering. But maybe it was true. And if they didn't know why I'd left, maybe they just didn't know me at all" (p.6-7).

It appears Harry's perception of events varies significantly from others in his family, who perhaps found a resilience to cope that Harry did not. Perhaps, influenced by symptoms of posttraumatic stress, MI, PB and his wife's perceptions too. He uses exaggerated language, to portray his sense of urgency, of grave peril and danger - the kind of statement a vulnerable victim of domestic abuse fleeing a violent perpetrator might make. Harry and Meghan had been planning to leave the UK since 2018 [130] and left in 2020. As multi-millionaires, they had significant funds behind them to support their move, purchase accommodation and furniture.

---

[130] (Sussex, 2022)

They left the UK on a private flight. Harry's claims seem dramatized rather than a true reflection of events.

Harry believes he is to "*wage a battle for* [Meghan's] *reputation and physical safety.*" Harry stated "*Someone* [reacted] *to what they'd read, had made a credible threat*" to her life. "*I might lose this woman*" (p.308). He believes the Press will not stop until Meghan is dead.[131] During an interview in 2021 Harry stated, "*my mother was chased to her death while she was in a relationship with someone that wasn't white, and now look what's happened – you want to talk about history repeating itself, they're not going to stop until [Meghan] dies.*" This distorted cognition was not mentioned in 'Spare.' Harry seems to be attempting to draw parallels between his life experience and his mother's, perhaps to share a common bond or connection with her.

---

[131] (Mountbatten-Windsor, 2021)

If Harry truly believes Meghan will die at the hands of the Press, it is little wonder that Meghan would begin to believe it too.

Harry stated he and Meghan fled the UK to escape the British tabloid press and the invasion of their privacy, to live in California. However, celebrities in California have similar issues with Paparazzi. Many are leaving to live elsewhere.

Justin Bieber accidentally hit a member of the paparazzi when he left church. Photographers took pictures of George and Amal Clooney's children inside their home by climbing their fence and hiding in a tree. Selena Gomez was pursued in her car by a photographer, causing an accident. Niall Horan was knocked to the ground by paparazzi as they rushed him, at L.A. International Airport. The paparazzi pursuit of Chris Brown resulted in his car being 'written off' in an accident. Sometimes the paparazzi are the ones getting injured, like the time Britney Spears drove over a photographer's foot when she was leaving a doctor's appointment. He was off work for six months.[132] Therefore, it seems Harry used the tabloid press as an excuse for leaving the UK, rather than a rational reason. If you want to escape the Press and paparazzi, California would not be your chosen destination.

During an interview, Meghan stated "*There was a lot of fear surrounding* [Archie, our son, having his photograph taken and published, as per Royal tradition]. *I was very scared of having to offer up our baby, knowing* [he wasn't] *going to be kept safe,*" which seems an overreaction and distorted cognition. This seems to be another excuse for not engaging with normal royal protocols. Yet, Harry and Meghan were happy to include video footage of their children at home in their docuseries.

Looking at a timeline of Harry's life, it appears he was largely out of the public eye. Harry was born on the 15th September 1984. He went to boarding school, during which time, there was an

---

[132] (Pajer, 2017)

agreement between the Royal family and the Press, that they would not intrude on Harry's privacy while he was in education. Therefore, Harry was protected from the Press by his family to a large extent. However, Harry exposed himself to negative Press coverage, when his issues with drugs and alcohol were revealed and he made poor judgements about his choice of a Nazi uniform for a fancy-dress party. He completed his education in 2003. A couple of years later, in 2005, he joined the army. Harry remained in the military for ten years, stating they were the happiest years of his life. He continued to receive protection from the intrusions of the Press during his military career. There were times when Harry's improper behaviour landed him in the newspapers. However, he stated he 'asked for it.' His reckless behaviour was perhaps associated with symptoms of PTSD. Harry did garner positive news coverage when he became founder of the Invictus Games in 2014 - supporting wounded and injured veterans with athletics.

After leaving the military in 2015, he was barely back to a quasi-civilian life before meeting Meghan Markle in 2016. He stated he did not know how to be a full time Royal when he left the military, nor was he sure it was what he wanted to be. He had never performed the duties of a senior Royal before. Meghan seemed to represent the escape route from the monarchy and the UK he wanted. Harry and Meghan were married in 2018, after a relatively brief courtship. Difficulties between Meghan and life within the British monarchy were apparent very soon after their wedding. Perhaps rather predictably, Harry and Meghan decided to leave the UK. They tried to leave in 2018, hoping to relocate to a commonwealth country[133] and finally abdicated from royal duties, emigrating in 2020. Since then, the Duke and Duchess of Sussex have pursued their own charitable and commercial ventures. On balance, any negative Press Harry has experienced personally, has been of his own

---

[133] (Sussex, 2022)

making and he has largely avoided a relationship with the Press at all. His perception of the Press as dangerous is clearly a result of the relationship between the tabloids and his mother, which according to Harry, caused her misery and ultimately death. His fears and anxieties about the Press were re-ignited following the introduction of new partners into his life and his wife, Meghan. All of whom came under scrutiny or criticism. Harry stated, the Press reinforced his desire to be 'anywhere but England' (p.200). During the preliminary hearing in High Court, London, against Associated Newspapers in March 2023; Harry stated he had feared his former girlfriend, Chelsy Davy, would be "harassed to death" by the Press when they were in a relationship.[134]

Harry and Meghan are partly responsible for the nature of the Press coverage they receive. Not only in the tabloids, but across all social media platforms. Harry targets the Press, because they

---

[134] (Sky-News, 2023)

are institutions that can be held accountable. He cannot sue everyone who speaks negatively about himself or Meghan. In fact, the greater threat and danger, lies in loosely controlled social media platforms where people can independently express their opinions. Meghan stated she was the most 'trolled' person in the world. [135] Research completed by a data intelligence agency (2021), stated there were 23% negative mentions in the US and 33% in the UK across online media. There were 28% negative mentions in the US and 33% in the UK across mainstream media. They found "*151,030 mentions across the month from all sources, spanning news, Twitter, blogs, videos and forums.*"[136] Therefore, Harry and Meghan (like the Royal family), have no control over Press and social media narratives. The best way to achieve positive Press, is to remain dignified, authentic, personable, and charitable.

---

[135] (Grierson, 2020)
[136] (Royston, 2021)

At present, it appears Harry and Meghan are promoting themselves as victims and seeking popularity through sympathy.

Institutional Betrayal & Organisational Injustice

"They didn't want Archie to be a prince and he wasn't going to receive security....the idea of our son not being safe, and also the idea of the first member of colour in this family not being titled in the same way that other grandchildren would be....." (Duchess of Sussex)

Institutional Betrayal is when *"common trusted and powerful institutions, [act] in ways that visit harm upon those dependent on them for safety and well-being."* [137] For example, harassment and insensitive investigations. Research explored the impact institutions may have on individuals following traumatic experience. Institutions may be responsible for a 'second assault' when one seeks help, including medical or judicial support. A victim of trauma may be stigmatized or blamed. There may be a 'closing of ranks' within an organisation seeking to protect its reputation, which is valued over and above the welfare of the

---

[137] (Freyd & Smith, 2013)

individual. Institutions can foster abuse. Research suggests that institutions may exacerbate post-traumatic reactions by contributing to existing trauma. The key factors are 'trust' and/or 'dependency' on the institution.[138] Betrayal has been found to predict dissociation and withdrawal in PTSD over and above the experience of fear, and fear does not significantly predict PTSD anxiety and arousal.[139] A sense of injustice, humiliation, betrayal, moral transgression and people in authority failing to do 'what's right,' are synonymous with MI and PB.

Being asked to make personal sacrifices morally, physically, emotionally and psychologically for what was believed to be a just cause - only to discover later this was not the case or personal sacrifices are not valued, may lead to feelings of betrayal. One may feel unsupported and even vilified for doing their job, by the very people who asked them to do it. Betrayal of one's trust can

---

[138] (Freyd & Smith, 2013)
[139] (Deprince, 2001)

have a long-lasting effect. Feelings of betrayal feature in MI, PB and PTSD. People may choose to be blind to betrayal, remain unaware or forget in order to protect a relationship which they may depend on for survival. [140] Examples could be where a child is dependent on an abusive caregiver, or where one is dependent on an institution for financial security. Harry and Meghan perceive institutional betrayal and the Royal family's blindness to it.

Harry stated, *"No institution is immune to accountability or taking responsibility. So, you can't be immune to criticisms either. My wife and I were scrutinized more than, probably, anybody else. I see a lack of scrutiny to my family towards a lot of the things that have happened in the last year. A symptom of one of the problems where we're not just talking about family relationships, we're talking about an antagonist, which is the British press, specifically the tabloids who want to create*

---

[140] (Freyd, 2019)

as much conflict as possible. The saddest part of that is certain members of my family and the people that work for them are complicit in that conflict."[141]

One interviewer posed the serenity prayer, often used in therapy, in an attempt to pose an alternative perspective on the position of the monarchy. He stated, *"give me serenity to accept what I can't change, the courage to change what I can and the wisdom to know the difference'* He stated Harry's family are *"on option 1, can't change the press, just accept it,* [Harry is] *on option 2, must do something about the press, if I don't stand up to what I consider abuses, no one else will."*[142]

Unfortunately, in his bid to reform the institutions, he has sought support from the wider world by exposing the moral transgressions he perceives and in doing so, he

---

[141] (Mohan-Hickson, 2023)
[142] (Mohan-Hickson, 2023)

has perpetrated the same behaviour that he accuses the monarchy of. Prince Harry continues to claim he would never leak against his family.[143] So how does he explain the leaked private conversations and moments in his memoir 'Spare,' involving his father, his stepmother, his brother and his sister-in-law? Just as Harry claims he is betrayed, he also betrays others who trusted him.

In relation to his family, Harry stated *"The ball is very much in their court, but, you know, Meghan and I have continued to say that we will openly apologize for anything that we did wrong, but every time we ask that question, no one's telling us the specifics or anything. There needs to be a constructive conversation, one that can happen in private that doesn't get leaked.* The interviewer speculated, *"I assume they would say, "Well, how can we trust you, how do we know that you're not going to reveal whatever conversations we have in*

---

[143] (Cooper, 2023)

an interview somewhere?" Having realised his own hypocrisy, Harry avoids answering the question and blames the Royal family. He seems to state two wrongs will make a right, implying 'They started it!' which perhaps demonstrates low emotional intelligence, which is a risk factor for developing MI and PB. He responded, *"This all started with them briefing, daily, against my wife with lies to the point of where my wife and I had to run away from my country.*[144] There is no evidence that Harry and Meghan needed to flee Britain. The Press and media attention, certainly has not waned since their departure, and is not likely to subside as long as the Duke and Duchess have a public profile and royal titles. Their decision to leave the UK and the monarchy was a lifestyle choice for them as a couple and not a result of danger.

---

[144] (Cooper, 2023)

Meghan claims organisational injustice at the withdrawal of protective security services when stepping down from official royal duties, lack of protection from the Press and failure to provide her with psychological support when she was struggling with her mental health.

During an interview, Meghan stated, *"I did anything they told me to do — of course I did, because it was also through the lens of, 'And we'll protect you'. So, even as things started to roll out in the media that I didn't see — but my friends would call me and say, 'Meg, this is really bad' — because I didn't see it, I'd go, 'Don't worry. I'm being protected'. I believed that. And I think that was... that was really hard to reconcile. It was only once we were married and everything started to really worsen that I came to understand that not only was I not being protected, but they were willing to lie to protect other members of the family but they weren't willing to tell the truth to protect me and my husband.* The interviewer asked, *"What kind of protection did you want that you feel you didn't receive?* Meghan replied, *"I mean, they would go on the record and negate the most ridiculous story for anyone, right? I'm talking about things that are super-artificial and inconsequential. But the narrative about, you know, making Kate cry, I think was the beginning of a real character assassination. And they knew it wasn't true. And I thought, well, if they're not going to kill things like that, then what are we going to do? It had never occurred to anyone that I wasn't OK...I was really suffering, and asked for help. That was when they were saying they didn't want Archie to be a prince and that he wasn't going to receive security.*

The interviewer asked, *"Was Archie being called a prince important to you?"* Meghan explained that *"If it meant he was going to be safe, then, of course. All the grandeur surrounding this stuff is an attachment that I don't personally have, right? I've been a waitress, an actress, a princess, a duchess. I've always just still been Meghan, right? So, for me, I'm clear on who I am, independent of all that stuff.*

And the most important title I will ever have is Mom. I know that. But the idea of our son not being safe, and also the idea of the first member of colour in this family not being titled in the same way that other grandchildren would be...You know, the other piece of that conversation is, there's a convention — I forget if it was George V or George VI convention — that when you're the grandchild of the monarch, so when Harry's dad becomes king, automatically Archie and our next baby would become prince or princess, or whatever they were going to be." The interviewer queried, *"and having the title gives you the safety and protection?"* Meghan's perception is *"Yes, but also it's not their right to take it away.* The interviewer stated, *"You know, we had heard — the world, those of us out here reading the things or hearing the things — that it was you and Harry who didn't want Archie to have a prince title. So, you're telling me that is not true?* Meghan responded, *"I, again, wouldn't wish pain on my child, but that is their birth-right for them to make a choice about."*[145]

The fact Meghan's first-born is biracial does not indicate Archie needs greater protection or that he would be denied a royal title because he is a baby 'of colour.' Meghan again appears to suggest institutional racism, where there is no evidence to support this perception. Harry is a Prince and has been refused publicly funded personal protection, and other members of the Royal family only have protection when on official duties. So, a title would not afford their children the protection Meghan has incorrectly assumed.

Harry and Meghan's children are unlikely to be working royals in the future, and so, would not need the title Prince and Princess. The Duke and Duchess of Wessex decided their children would not use royal titles, as they would most likely need to work as private citizens to support themselves. Princess Anne's children have no royal titles

---

[145] (Markle M., 2021)

either. Harry and Meghan have no right to accuse the monarchy of treating them unfavourably or disadvantaging them in any way. Few royals have round-the-clock security and protection, despite their royal status.[146]

In 'Spare' Harry states *"we were prepared to make any sacrifice necessary to find some peace and safety, including relinquishing our Sussex titles"* (p.378). Yet, he will be aware that even if the titles Duke and Duchess of Sussex are removed, they would then be known as Prince and Princess. If Harry were to renounce his peerage, they could become Mr and Mrs Harry Mountbatten-Windsor. According to the Peerage Act 1963, renouncing titles shall be irrevocable and will *"divest that person (and, if he is married, his wife) of all right or interest to or in the peerage, and all titles, rights, offices, privileges and precedence attaching*

---

146 (Duell, 2021)

thereto; and to relieve him of all obligations and disabilities arising therefrom."[147]

It is unlikely Harry will request the removal of his titles. Harry and Meghan will be acutely aware they will have significantly less earning power without their royal status.

Harry is not the only Royal in modern times or in history to break with a monarchy. In 2022, Jordan's Prince Hamzah bin Hussein renounced his title *"because his convictions cannot be reconciled with the 'approaches, policies and methods of [Jordanian] institutions'."* He too, was involved in a 'palace feud,' and a family rift. Royal analyst, Sabaileh stated, *"He is trying to re-engage with the old narrative. We are back to the point where he is saying he is not satisfied; that he is still bitter and there is no reconciliation."*[148] Harry has yet to take the step of stripping away his titles for his principles.

---

[147] (Gov.uk, 2023)
[148] (Aljazeera, 2022)

Meghan sought help from the institution when her mental health became a concern. She stated *"I just didn't want to be alive any more. And that was a very clear and real and frightening constant thought. And I remember how he just cradled me. And I went to the institution, and I said that I needed to go somewhere to get help. I said that, 'I've never felt this way before, and I need to go somewhere'. And I was told that I couldn't, that it wouldn't be good for the institution. And so, I went to human resources, and I said, 'I just really — I need help'. Because in my old job, there was a union, and they would protect me. And I remember this conversation like it was yesterday, because they said, 'My heart goes out to you, because I see how bad it is, but there's nothing we can do to protect you because you're not a paid employee of the institution'.*

This wasn't a choice. This was emails and begging for help, saying very specifically, 'I am concerned for my mental welfare'. And people going, 'Oh, yes, yes, it's disproportionately terrible what we see out there to anyone else'. But nothing was ever done, so we had to find a solution. It was very clear and very scary. And, you know, I didn't know who to even turn to in that. And one of the people that I reached out to, who's continued to be a friend and confidant, was one of my husband's mom's best friends, one of Diana's best friends. Because it's, like, who else could understand what it's actually like on the inside? You couldn't just go. You couldn't. I mean, you have to understand, as well, when I joined that family, that was the last time, until we came here, that I saw my passport, my driver's licence, my keys. All that gets turned over. I didn't see any of that anymore." The interviewer stated, *"Well, the way you're describing this, it...it's like you were trapped and couldn't get help, even though you're on the verge of suicide. That's what you are describing. That's what I'm hearing.*[149]

---

[149] (Markle M. , 2021)

Meghan implies she was held prisoner, unable to get help or escape. Her car keys, driving licence, passport – all confiscated. Yet, this does not correlate with the fact Harry and Meghan left the UK without any obstruction, were not met with any resistance and allegedly 'fled' the country (presumably with their necessary documentation).

Meghan struggles to understand why she and her husband were not accommodated with a hybrid working model within the monarchy, that would enable them to perform official duties part-time whilst living outside the UK. She stated, "*We never left the family and we only wanted to have the same type of role that exists, right? There are senior members of the family and then there are non-senior members. And we said, specifically, 'We're stepping back from senior roles to be just like several...' I mean, I can think of so many right now who are all... they're royal highnesses, prince or princess, duke or duchess... who earn a living, live on palace grounds, can support the Queen if and when called upon. So, we weren't reinventing the wheel here. We were saying, 'OK, if this isn't working for everyone, we're in a lot of pain, you can't provide us with the help we need, we can just take a step back. We can do it in a Commonwealth country'. We suggested New Zealand, South Africa...*"[150]

Harry and Meghan suggest they could represent the monarchy within the Commonwealth, particularly as Meghan is biracial, which they believe would be welcomed. However, this does seem a rather patronising assumption to make. The future of the commonwealth and the Royal family's involvement in it is unclear. The commonwealth is changing and the monarchy may step back from *"one of the world's biggest international organisations, made up of 54 countries, almost all of which were former colonies of the United Kingdom."* Philip Murphy, professor of British and Commonwealth History at the

---

[150] (Markle M. , 2021)

University of London, stated "*I think perhaps the Commonwealth has historically run its course, and what you're really seeing now is the ghost of an organisation. It will just gradually become less influential, less important and less interesting to its citizens.*" Some are of the opinion that the Royal family should not lead the Commonwealth going forward, since the death of Queen Elizabeth II, who created the organisation. Furthermore, this would likely be a senior Royal role.[151] The author posits that whoever takes up the mantle of the Commonwealth will need to do so with humility and not use the position for self-serving reasons.

Harry's beliefs were shattered when his full-time protection was withdrawn as a result of his exit from the monarchy. He stated "*I never thought that I would have my security removed, because I was born into this position. I inherited the risk. So that was a shock to me. That was what completely changed the whole plan.*"

---

[151] (Mills, 2022)

Meghan stated "*My regret is believing them when they said I would be protected. I believed that. And I regret believing that because I think, 'had I really seen that wasn't happening, I would have been able to do more'. But I think I wasn't supposed to see it. I wasn't supposed to know. And... and now, because we're actually on the other side, we've actually not just survived but are thriving.*"[152] It seems while their departure from the monarchy and the UK may have been distressing for them, Harry and Meghan recognise they are happier for the move. Hopefully, they will have the wisdom to perceive that every cloud has a silver lining, and to not continue public punishment of the monarchy, perhaps taking some accountability for their own perceptions, behaviour and decisions.

---

[152] (Markle M. , 2021)

Querulous Litigant

"I am moving the mission of changing the media landscape from being personal, to my life's work" (Duke of Sussex)

A 'Querulous Litigant' relentlessly pursues a sense of justice through legal means, often disproportionate to the offence, driven by a desire to be vindicated and reform institutions through social action or as a means of revenge. Querulous delusion may lead to a querulous litigant – the primary symptom is embitterment and distorted perceptions, usually regarding blame. [153] Querulous behaviour is often associated with MI and PB.

Harry appears to be a querulous litigant. He disclosed his three pending cases of litigation against the Press. [154] According to one media source The Duke and Duchess of Sussex launched six legal cases between September 2019 and

---

[153] (Carter, 2021)
[154] (Mohan-Hickson, 2023)

November 2020.[155] A further case of litigation was initiated and appeared publicly in January 2022. Harry made a claim against the Home Office and RAVEC (Royal and VIP Executive Committee) regarding the withdrawal of his personal protection and security services since his abdication from royal duties in 2020.

All cases of litigation relate to Harry's perception of danger, his fears that history will repeat itself and his feelings of institutional betrayal or organisational injustice. He fears losing his wife, as he lost his mother. Harry seems genuinely terrified he will suffer the same trauma, believing his mother was killed by the Press and because she did not have official security services protecting her at the time of her death. Harry is desperately trying to control these perceived threats. Harry illuminates his mental state when stating *"I huddled with the lawyer, trying to work out how to protect Meg. I spent most of every day,*

---

[155] (Royston, 2022)

from the moment I opened my eyes until long past midnight, trying to make it stop. Sue them, I kept telling the lawyer, over and over" (p.299-300). Harry stated, *"my own countrymen, and countrywomen, showing such contempt, such vile disrespect to the woman I loved. Sometimes, I'd asked for it, but this woman has done nothing to deserve such cruelty"* (p.310).

Psychological injury may develop from both a weak belief in a just world and an experience of injustice. The 'just world hypothesis' is a belief one gets what they deserve and deserves what they get. This belief is challenged or undermined by negative life events. One may feel unable to adjust to new beliefs or continue on as before. One may experience great distress trying to understand why something has happened.[156]

The expectation of 'just deserts,' is perhaps more significant to individuals exposed to risks that are out of their control, such as fate, which is arguably

---

[156] (Carter, 2020)

a reflection of Harry's life. The experience of injustice only has a negative effect on the individual, when the level of adversity is too great to be assimilated into the psyche. Ones' strong belief in a 'just world' is not undermined by exposure to violence. It is shattered by betrayal and injustice which can be destabilizing to one's belief in personal worth or value.[157]

After the acquittal of former tabloid executive Rebekah Brooks in the phone hacking scandal, (2014), Harry stated "*my faith in the whole* [judicial] *system took a serious hit when that woman got off scot-free. I needed a reset, a faith refresher*" (p.242).

Harry's comment demonstrates shattered beliefs and a loss of faith in an otherwise trusted institution. An institution relied upon for the protection of the innocent and the punishment of harm-doers - a significant example of MI and PB.

---

[157] (Carter, 2020)

Harry's memoir is his revenge against the press, those he believes colluded with them (his wider family) and the monarchy as an institution. He uses 'Spare' as a platform for exposing the harm he perceives himself to suffer and 'show the world' who the 'villains' are, including his desire for justice. He states *"They asked about my hacking lawsuit. Still ongoing. Suicide mission, Pa mumbled. Maybe. But it's worth it. I'd soon prove that the press were more than liars, I said. That they were lawbreakers. I was going to see some of them thrown into gaol. It wasn't about me, it was a matter of public interest,"* (p.396) *"In announcing the lawsuit I laid out my case to the world"* (p.424).

Harry was overjoyed when Press editors and reporters were arrested for harassment. He stated, *"corruption was being exposed, finally, and punishments were forthcoming. Soon enough they would all lose their jobs, and their ill-gotten fortunes, amassed during one of the wildest crime sprees in British history."* Harry used keywords associated with MI and PB, such as betrayal, validation, vindication and justice to describe his feelings (p.167). However, he may not feel satiated by this victory because the justice he truly seeks is the imprisonment of the Press for the death of his mother. He states *"why were those [paparazzi] not more roundly blamed. Why were they not in gaol"* (p.132).

The fact Harry has relinquished privacy and 'normality' which he states is *"the one resource more precious than water"* (p.90), in favour of multiple cases of litigation and a tell-all memoir to the world, may indicate symptoms of MI and PB. The fight for justice and vindication can become all-consuming to the detriment of relationships, occupation and financial security - the risk of significant or total loss is high, if one cannot let go of the grudge, the fight, the principal, the idealistic view point.[158]

---

[158] (Carter, 2021)

Harry's reaction to the Press was immediate very soon after his relationship with Meghan became public. According to Harry, controversial articles began to appear soon after his relationship with Meghan had been disclosed. Rather than wait for the situation to settle down and to cooperate with the Press, Harry went on the offensive. The lawyer explained to sue the papers would be a confirmation of Harry's relationship with Meghan and then they could 'really go to town' reporting on her. The advice Harry was given is that he would be 'feeding the beast.' Silence is the best option. Harry stated silence was not an option (p.300). He abandoned the Royal stance of 'never complain, never explain,'[159] which has served the monarchy well. Harry does not agree with their view point. He stated his family's silence is a betrayal.[160] As predicted, Harry's statement to the Press in November 2016 in defence of Meghan, ignited an onslaught of Press attention.

---

[159] (Mohan-Hickson, 2023)
[160] (Mohan-Hickson, 2023)

In May 2018, The Mail on Sunday, published a story stating Meghan's father, Mr Markle had staged candid photos with the help of the paparazzi for money. Mr Markle denied this was true when challenged by Meghan. She later discovered he was indeed lying about his involvement with the Press. She had been betrayed by her own father. A couple of months later (August 2018) Meghan sent her father a letter in the post, claiming she was unable to meet with him in person. The letter was leaked to the Press and published. The Duchess of Sussex took the newspaper to court over privacy and copyright breaches.[161]

However, Harry stated "[Meghan] *had always known it might be intercepted, but she never stopped to think her father would actually offer it*" (p.356). Perhaps this was entirely predictable given that Mr Markle had sold photographs to the Press only months before. Harry stated after this

---

[161] (BBC-News, 2021)

breach of privacy, he *"didn't want to hear any more talk of protocols, tradition, strategy"* (p.356). This was the final straw – the catalyst for instigating private legal action. The Duchess has come under criticism from the publishers, stating "[the letter] *was written with an awareness it could be made public. It was crafted with the possibility of public consumption in mind."* Lawyers for the newspaper submitted a witness statement from Meghan and Harry's communications secretary, including text messages between them about drafting the letter to Mr Markle. They discussed whether the letter should be *"addressed to 'daddy.' In the unfortunate event [the letter is] leaked, it would pull at the heartstrings. The letter is real, honest and factual and if he leaks it, then that's on his conscience, and at least the world will know the truth. Words I could never voice publicly."*[162] Contrary to Harry's statement that Meghan never dreamt her father

---

[162] (Coughlan, 2021)

would be the one to leak the letter, Meghan clearly stated the possibility was on her mind. It seems Meghan was determined to hold the Press to account for publishing content she actually wanted people to see and read.

Harry and Meghan were not only focused on taking the Press to court. Harry requested a judicial review of some decisions made by RAVEC (Royal and VIP Executive Committee), concerning arrangements for police to provide the duke with publicly funded personal security when he is in Great Britain. RAVEC membership consists of Home Office officials, Metropolitan police and those who work within the Royal household. On the 24th March 2022, the judge agreed to allow the case to progress to a review of some (not all) of the grounds made by the claimant (Harry).[163]

Harry had ceased to become a working member of the Royal family in April 2020. He relocated to Canada and then to America. Queen Elizabeth II

---

[163] (Swift, 2022)

changed his role to a privately-funded member of the Royal family, with permission to earn his own income and pursue his own private charitable interests. Therefore, Harry no longer undertakes representative duties on behalf of the monarchy.

RAVEC will provide protection to VIPs and members of the Royal family if they fall within one of four categories. 1) protection is provided to persons as a matter of course, regardless of threat and risk, because of the position they hold, 2) protection is provided to other persons if RAVEC determines this is a proportionate response to a risk assessment of likelihood of an attack and impact of successful attack, 3) protection is provided on a case-by-case basis and 4) is redacted and not provided for public consumption.

RAVEC have assessed the Duke of Sussex as falling under category two, because he no longer lives in Great Britain full time and an assessment of risk and threat, only needs to be made when RAVEC is made aware he intends to visit the UK. Furthermore, that the provision of protection would be dependent on the nature of the visit.[164] For example, visiting family would not necessarily require publicly funded police protection in addition to his own privately funded security. Whereas, a state affair, such as the King's coronation may increase the likelihood of attack, and greater intelligence input into the assessment of risk and threat. One may venture Harry's inflammatory comments in 'Spare' regarding his Taliban kill count, with the upcoming King's coronation could be an example of heightened risk, which would need to be accommodated. RAVEC intends to monitor threats to Harry and undertake dynamic risk assessments. If an issue were to arise, RAVEC would take appropriate action. They are of the opinion there is no basis for publicly funded security for the Duke and Duchess of Sussex when they visit Great Britain. RAVEC suggest Harry

---

[164] (Swift, 2022)

communicates his private arrangements for security when he is in the UK, so they can review if any additional security is warranted. However, it is of note that Prince Harry made a surprise visit to London to attend the High Court in March 2023, regarding his joint litigation against Associated Newspapers. It appears he did not notify the government of his visit or seek protection from RAVEC security services [165] which perhaps undermines his case and his argument. His behaviour indicates his claim against RAVEC is disingenuous. Only a year before, Harry had told the court he should fall under category one, stating he has had publicly funded security since birth and it is his birth-right as sixth in line to the throne.[166]

Harry tenuously attempted to link his position in the line of succession, outlined in the 'Succession of the Crown Act 2013' stating he was required to ask HM Queen Elizabeth II for permission to

---

[165] (Nanan-Sen, 2023)
[166] (Swift, 2022)

marry and therefore, protection should be provided as a matter of course because of the position he holds. The judge refused this ground for review, stating the legislation he refers to is not applicable to this case. Harry's second ground of complaint, is that RAVEC should have taken into consideration that 'he sought' to remain a working member of the Royal family, undertaking part-time duties, with occasional representation on behalf of HM Queen Elizabeth II. The judge refused this claim because Harry was aware the hybrid model of working, he proposed, had been declined by the Queen as an unrealistic option.

The judge has permitted a judicial review on the grounds that Harry was not made aware of RAVEC protocol or policy, he had not had an opportunity to comment on RAVEC's risk assessment and Harry believes the decision made by RAVEC in relation to his UK visits in February 2020 and July 2021 were unreasonable. Harry challenges whether RAVEC considered risk, and made reasonable enquiries to inform their assessment prior to his UK visit for the funeral of Prince Philip (2021). RAVEC will have an opportunity to present their risk assessment documentation to the judicial review. The most significant ground Harry submits to the court for judicial review, in terms of potential querulous delusion, is Harry's assertion that the process of risk assessment was bias. Harry demonstrates suspiciousness, cynicism and distrust. He complains he was not made aware of the involvement and membership of 'certain individuals' within RAVEC. According to one press release, the cabinet office is a member of RAVEC. The cabinet secretary (Britain's most senior civil servant) is Simon Case – formerly Prince William's private secretary.[167] It appears Harry suspects foul play regarding the withdrawal of his publicly funded security, instigated by his brother, William. However, the judge stated there is no evidence to support

---

[167] (Royston, 2023)

Harry's claim of bias.[168] Harry stated in 'Spare' "*I pleaded for continuation of the same armed police protection I'd had, and needed, since birth. I'd never been allowed to go anywhere without three armed bodyguards, even when I was supposedly the most popular member of the family, and now I was the target, along with my wife and son, of unprecedented hate*" (p.382).

Harry stated he would pay for police protection in the UK. However, there is no option for him to do so. Harry's perception of threat level may have been influenced by his bodyguard who stated "*the threat level was still higher than for that of nearly every other royal, equal to that assigned the Queen*" (p.387). Perhaps the issue is not whether protection is needed, but who will provide it and pay for it. Harry stated "*the palace directed me to a firm, which quoted me a price [of] six million a year*" (p. 387). Harry's distorted perception of danger, coupled with having close protection for

---

[168] (Swift, 2022)

as long as he can remember, led him to challenge the decision to withdrawal security services.

However, most senior royals only have protection when carrying out royal duties and Harry no longer represents the monarchy. He is now a private citizen. Zara Tindall, Princess Beatrice, Princess Eugenie and Prince Andrew have no publicly funded security. Princess Anne, Prince Edward and his wife Sophie are only given protection on official duties. [169] Therefore, it would seem RAVEC have appropriately assessed Harry's security needs. Harry and Meghan have not been treated unfavourably, nor through bias.

Persistent complainants are significantly less likely to consider their complaint resolved at the point of closure of their case, more likely to seek public acknowledgment of their mistreatment and an apology, as well as demands for the dismissal or prosecution of those responsible. *"More extreme forms of revenge, such as public*

---

[169] (Duell, 2021)

exposure and humiliation, were demanded exclusively by the persistent complainant." Persistent complainants were more likely to demand justice on matters of principle and *"insisted on their day in court."*[170] The querulent person may have obsessional, paranoid or narcissistic personality.[171] Harry's querulousness (once a diagnosable syndrome of a delusional nature), seems to shout from the pages of Harry's memoir and media interviews, as well as MI, PTSD and PB. Harry displays symptoms associated with these conditions, such as distorted perceptions about the cause or consequences of the trauma, feeling betrayed, vengeance, self- destructive behaviour, negative beliefs about self, danger seeking, blame, shame, guilt, anger, embitterment, rumination, feelings of humiliation and injustice, avoidance, rigid perceptions and difficulty with forgiveness. (Carter, 2020)

---

[170] (Lester, Wilson, Griffin, & Mullen, 2004)
[171] (Carter, 2020)

Reporting for the BBC, Rajan and Lee (2021), stated Harry "*has so far declined to settle his phone-hacking claim, raising the prospect of a trial,*"[172] which further substantiates symptoms of PB, the need to publicly humiliate and expose the perpetrator, to feel vindicated - to no longer be a powerless victim, to 'have his day in court.' To further demonstrate Harry's querulous litigiousness, on the 27th March 2023, he flew to London from the US to attend the aforementioned preliminary hearing of the phone hacking case involving him and other claimants. The preliminary hearing determines if there is a case to answer. News footage showed Harry accidentally collide with a press photographer outside court, and if he had personal protection with him, they certainly weren't protecting him from the close proximity of the press. [173] His behaviour suggests his need to engage with

---

[172] (Rajan & Lee, 2021)

[173] (Nanan-Sen, 2023)

litigation, outweighs his fears and anxieties of perceived danger or flying into London.

Revenge fantasy may be in response to persistent and prolonged abuse, threat, betrayal or trauma, where there is a sense of not being able to escape the situation and powerlessness to stop the abuse of power. Revenge fantasy which may be graphic, violent and pleasurable may seem like a kind of antidote to feelings of powerlessness and victimisation. *"The roles of perpetrator and victim are reversed.....the victim imagines that revenge is the only way to restore one's own sense of power, and may also imagine that this is the only way to force the perpetrator to acknowledge the harm...done."* (Herman, 1997: 189) [174] It is important to replace revenge fantasy with an alternative path to justice - such as court action, peer support, raising public awareness, being heard and having one's experiences validated, which Harry appears to do. However, the focus

---

[174] (Herman, 1997)

needs to be overcoming *"the preoccupation with the traumatic event,* [and] *to give up the right to continuously punish the person who has 'wronged' the victim...." (Linden & Maercker, 2011:123)*[175]

Even though Harry left the UK believing this would stop the Press from reporting on him and his wife, he discovered this was not the case. He stated *"I left the country and for twelve months it was relentless. So again, one of the reasons why I am moving the mission of changing the media landscape within the UK from being personal to my life's work, a large part of that is down to the ongoing legal battles.*

Specifically, with phone hacking. I put in my claims over three years ago. And I'm still waiting. One might assume that a lot of this, from their perspective, is retaliation, and trying to intimidate me to settle, rather than take it to court and potentially have to shut down." The interviewer

---

[175] (Linden & Maercker, 2011)

stated, *"Phone hacking happened a decade ago, three cases, which are very rarely referred to against News Group which you know, may or may not come to court, you've got a case against the Mirror which may or may not come to court and you've – with others including Doreen Lawrence (Stephen Lawrence's mum), you've taken a case against the Mail. I have to say, in all three cases the accusations are very grave and the stakes I would say are very high, I mean I would say certainly like the Mail you're suggesting they hired private investigators to break into people's houses to plant a listening device, I mean this is off the scale, they deny it absolutely.* Harry stated *"if they want to hold us and the rich and powerful to account, and they want to police society, then who's policing* [the Press]*? I don't know how long it's going to take, but it is 100% worth it.*[176] The interviewer stated *"if it's not a horrible article in a newspaper it's going to be out there on* [social media]*, so what your family might say to you is 'Look, you you've got to*

---

[176] (Mohan-Hickson, 2023)

let it go – you can't fight it all.' I understand your narrative is 'I [must] *stand up to what I believe ...'* *but isn't there a danger that given your background and trauma, you're maybe not taking the most logical view of this, as in you're permanently at war and seeing the media as one entity?* Harry responded *"No I'm not permanently at war at all. I made peace with it; I was willing to let a lot of it go back in 2020 when we left the country. And if living in a new country, minding our own business during lockdown, not saying anything, not doing anything that would affect the British media at all, that every single day there's an, attack, well then, the assumption of it going away or moving on isn't the case.*

So, you know, I feel as though there is a responsibility to see this through, because I think the benefits to a lot of people will be felt [177]

Harry claims there should have been no reason for the Press to report on him and his family

---

[177] (Mohan-Hickson, 2023)

during lockdown, stating they weren't saying anything or doing anything of interest.[178] Harry's notion is surprising. He and Meghan had just fled the UK and abdicated from royal duties at the same time as the Covid-19 lockdown in 2020. Does Harry really believe this would not be cause for a media frenzy? Harry and Meghan announced they were stepping back from royal duties in January 2020. The first lockdown in the UK was March 2020. Harry and Meghan relocated to California in March 2020. April 2020, they *"announced they would no longer engage with or respond to inquiries from journalists from the Sun, the Daily Mail, the Daily Mirror, and the Daily Express, explaining they no longer wished to "offer themselves up as currency for an economy of clickbait and distortion."* [179] Harry and Meghan also announced the launch of their non-profit company 'Archewell' in the same month. In September 2020, Harry and Meghan announce

---

[178] (Mohan-Hickson, 2023)
[179] (McDowell, 2022)

the creation of their own production company and signed a deal with Netflix and in November 2020, Meghan published a piece in the New York Times about a miscarriage she sadly experienced with her husband in July 2020.[180] These are big news stories and of significant interest to the public. Harry's statement that they were doing and saying nothing does not correlate with the evidence.

---

[180] (McDowell, 2022)

Delusion of grandeur

"Reconciliation between my family and us will have a ripple effect across the entire world" (Duke of Sussex)

Harry's strategy is to single-handedly reform the monarchy and the tabloid Press, as an outsider of both institutions - fighting on two fronts simultaneously. However, this is one man's mission against an ancient institution, whose reigning monarchs must be getting things right. There is a reason the monarchy has endured in Britain. The monarchy continues to have the love, support and respect of the people of Britain, the Commonwealth and the world - demonstrated by an outpouring of respect from the people - mourning the death of Queen Elizabeth II on the 8th September 2022.

Harry's interview with the Telegraph newspaper since the launch of his published memoir, demonstrated what appears to be saviour complex and delusion of grandeur.

Harry attempts to justify his narrative by using Prince William's children as the motivation for his mission to reform the monarchy. "*The Duke revealed that he felt "responsibility" to reform the monarchy for the sake of Prince George, nine, Princess Charlotte, seven, and Prince Louis, four. "This is not about trying to collapse the monarchy – this is about trying to save them from themselves,"* Harry's uncompromising pursuit of justice (*"his "technique"*), *he suggested, was to completely curtail the relationship between the Royal family and the Press and, by doing so, protect them*"[181] Yet, Harry seems unlikely to ever curtail his own relationship with the Press, not even to protect himself and his own psychological health, which is a hypocritical stance. Furthermore, he has no right to dictate whether or not members of the Royal family engage with the Press or forge a mutually beneficial relationship – one which could limit any damage to reputation or invasion

---

[181] (Wood, 2023)

of privacy and enable the monarchy to have some control and management of Press releases. Amol Rajan (journalist) stated, the Windsor family get to live in a palace, they get some taxpayer funding, in return for granting access and providing a steady supply of photos and stories to the Press. This is in exchange for favourable coverage, which enables the Royal family to renew their emotional contract with the public. This only works if both parties stick to their side of the bargain – that's the deal.[182]

In a television interview Harry implied he feels a bitterness toward more senior members of the Royal family for using the Press to steal the limelight. This suggests he perceives himself to be of greater importance, regardless of the hierarchy within the monarchy. Harry is aware of the royal protocol. There should be no competition for press coverage where more senior Royals hold events and perform official duties. Harry is

---

[182] (Rajan, The Princes and the Press, 2021)

particularly critical of Camilla's press attention. He stated, during an interview *"She was the villain. [Camilla] was the third person in their marriage. She needed to rehabilitate her image."* The interviewer stated *"You wrote that she started a campaign in the British press to pave the way for a marriage. And you wrote, "I even wanted Camilla to be happy. Maybe she'd be less dangerous if she was happy."* The interviewer asked, *"How was she dangerous? Because of the need for her to rehabilitate her image? That made her dangerous?"* Harry replied *"That made her dangerous because of the connections that she was forging within the British press. And there was open willingness on both sides to trade of information. And with a family built on hierarchy, and with her, on the way to being Queen consort, there was going to be people or bodies left in the street because of that".*

The interviewer commentated, stating *"Harry says over the years, he was one of those bodies. He accuses Camilla and even his father, at times, of using him or William to get better tabloid coverage for themselves. Prince Harry writes, Camilla, "sacrificed me on her personal P.R. altar." Harry explained, "If you are led to believe, as a member of the family, that being on the front page, having positive headlines, positive stories written about you, is going to improve your reputation or increase the chances of you being accepted as monarch by the British public, then that's what you're going to do."*[183]

Harry's perception of Camilla, seems to be a projection of his own behaviour and desire for Press attention. He believes Camilla is a danger to him, because she is competition for his own publicity. He relies on press coverage for self-identity and to feed his Press addiction. It's almost as if the Royal family are getting between him and his 'fix.' This is causing him to lash out at his family. However, Harry is in fact a danger to the monarchy because of his unpredictable behaviour and betrayal of their trust.

---

[183] (Cooper, 2023)

Despite this, Harry wishes to have a relationship with his father, brother and sister-in-law. In an interview, Harry stated *"reconciliation between my family and us will have a ripple effect across the entire world."* [184] which seems to suggest a delusion of grandeur and self-importance. While the public may be somewhat relieved to see Harry reunited with his family, it isn't going to affect their day to day lives. People are more concerned about the current 'cost of living crisis' in the UK, the war in Ukraine and global issues, such as climate change. People are perhaps curious about the Harry and Meghan scandal, as they are with any other celebrity. The Duke and Duchess certainly present as two altruistic, kind, decent individuals, who are deeply in love. But, neither of them seems to be uniquely talented or inspirational. Nor in the same league as great speakers, motivators, activists, scientists or philosophers.

---

[184] (Mohan-Hickson, 2023)

In his TV interview, Harry stated the docuseries and the memoir 'Spare;' *"Were necessary, they were essential, for historical fact and significance"* [185] Yet, Harry does not present historical fact. He offers his version of events.

It is difficult to see how writing his memoir, launching a docuseries and holding TV interviews would keep Meghan safe and not expose her to further negative Press, abusive threats and danger. Harry seems more concerned with other, more senior members of the Royal family getting greater attention than himself from the Press. Harry stated *"One of the main reasons for [leaving the UK] was to remove ourselves from this competition that was happening for the front pages."* He goes on to justify his actions by stating *"over the last six years, the level of planting and leaking from other members of the family means that in my mind they have written countless books, certainly millions of words have been dedicated to*

---

[185] (Mohan-Hickson, 2023)

trying to trash my wife and myself to the point of where I had to leave my country."[186] Is Harry really that important? Are the Royal family really that preoccupied with manipulating the downfall of Prince Harry, the King's 'darling boy' and alleged favourite of Queen Elizabeth II. It seems unlikely.

---

[186] (Mohan-Hickson, 2023)

Autobiographical memory

"As a defence mechanism, most likely, my memory was no longer recording things quite as it once did"

(Duke of Sussex)

Perhaps the most surprising observation is not what is included in the book, but what is missing. In particular, the absence of Harry's mother. Where was Diana during his childhood? There are some references to her, such as her favourite pudding, the brand of beauty cream she used, places they would go on holiday, the time they spent with their mother on military exercise with the Special Boat Service (SBS) in the 'killing house.' What was less evident, were parent-child interactions. Harry stated he could not recall his mother holding him, giving him a hug or a cuddle (p.254). However, he writes fondly and frequently of time spent with his father, servants, bodyguards, school friends, school matrons and his Nanny. He refers to his Nanny (Tiggy), as his mother's rival.

He describes his strong affection for her. Harry appears to view his mother through the eyes of the world, as a pure person of light who helped so many people in need. As omnipresent (p.3) and a deity. As if he were an outside observer on this relationship. Harry stated *"she would sometimes over-mother, then disappear for stretches"* (p.311), implying in the brief time they were together, Diana was over compensating for all the time they were apart. Was Diana an absent mother? Or is her absence in Harry's memoir a testament to emotional numbing and repressed memories? Harry states, *"Despite my clear memory of not wanting to remember her, I was also trying gamely not to forget her* (P.48)," which perhaps signifies both rumination and avoidance associated with complicated grief and MI.

Many types of loss are features of MI and PB. For example, loss of beliefs, meaning and purpose, trust, personal identity, family or friends, security, future orientation, self-esteem, career or vocation and significant personal investment (sacrifices). The loss which results from an injustice and violation of one's deeply held values, morals and beliefs can touch multiple areas of one's life. Grief is a process of trying to assimilate and accept loss. One learns to live with the experience rather than continue to live in the experience. For some, embitterment reactions, similar to complicated grief are enduring. *"There are grievers who do not want the grief to end, as they feel it is all that is left of the relationship with their loved one."* and they fluctuate between rumination and avoidance of reminders. [187] Embittered people are not sure they want the wounds to heal. [188] Harry stated, the pain associated with the loss of his mother is all he has left of her. The pain is his driver, his motivation and *"some days the pain is the only thing holding [him] together"* (p.309).

---

[187] (Zisook & Shear, 2009)
[188] (Linden, Rotter, & Schippan, 2007)

The experience of complicated grief goes through various stages and can include: disbelief, shock, numbness, denial that the loss or change is happening, anger and blame directed at others, feelings of bitterness or resentment, feeling vulnerable or helpless, sadness, confusion, hurt, avoiding emotions by trying to stay in control, withdrawal from others, guilt, treating others negatively, acceptance that this has happened and finding ways to live with the experience and move forward. [189] *"The disruption associated with bereavement can trigger various disorders, including not only Prolonged Grief Disorder but also major depression and posttraumatic stress disorder (PTSD).[190]* Harry felt he had lost almost all of himself to grief and the paparazzi (p.96).

Following therapy, Harry stated he began to remember more of his mother. Though these memories still seem to lack parent-child interactions. He recalls time with his mother in

---

[189] (Litz, Lebowitz, Gray, & Nash, 2016)
[190] (Jordan & Litz, 2014)

the company of others, at work, or in the presence of paparazzi. He remembers saying goodnight to her downstairs and feeling alone in his bedroom, in the dark and the silence, (furthest away from his mother's room). He does not speak of bedtime stories and being tucked into bed, or the soft glow from a nightlight his mother left on for him, or songs she might sing while he drifted off to sleep. Even the car journeys to tennis lessons were intercepted by paparazzi (p.313-314). In contrast, despite Harry's criticism of his father as a single parent, he stated *"I'd shout downstairs, going to bed, Pa! He'd shout back cheerfully – I'll be there shortly, darling boy! True to his word, minutes later he'd be sitting on the edge of my bed. He never forgot that I didn't like the dark, so he'd gently tickle my face until I fell asleep. I have the fondest memories of his hands on my cheeks, my forehead, then waking to find him gone, magically, the door always considerately left open a crack"* (p.31).

There are many examples where Harry cannot recall life events with certainty. *"Alas, the memory lies, with a million others, on the other side of a high mental wall. Such a horrid, tantalizing feeling, to know they're over there, just on the other side, mere inches away—but the wall is always too high, too thick. Unscalable (p.11). "Am I remembering this correctly?" (p.102). "As a defence mechanism, most likely, my memory was no longer recording things quite as it once did"* (p.27).

"Research has found that an individual who has been diagnosed with a mental health disorder may have a distorted perception of reality, and what they feel is correct about their lives, may not be an accurate reflection of what is actually occurring. In turn, this could mean that an individual with a mental health disorder could have issues when being asked to recall autobiographical events and they may recall events in an unclear way." [191]

---

[191] (Jenkins, 2023)

Harry stated he does not consider himself to have a disorder and prefers the term Post Traumatic Stress Injury (PTSI). [192] A term used to reduce stigma and recognise that people can continue to function with a psychological injury. Perhaps Harry's memory loss is trauma related, or perhaps his memory has been affected by the use of illicit drugs, or both. Had his mother been a significant and integral part of his childhood, one would expect evidence of this in Harry's memoir. *"Under some circumstances, false memories for autobiographical events can be implanted."* In cases of repeated victimisation, false memories could significantly impact the person's life narrative.[193] Therefore, Harry's recollections may not be an accurate or true reflection of events.

---

[192] (Mohan-Hickson, 2023)
[193] (Calado, Luke, Deborah, Landstrom, & Otgaar, 2021)

Healing from trauma

"It felt like I was turning pain into a purpose"
(Duke of Sussex)

Harry stated in an interview, "*My military career saved me in many regards. It got me out of the spotlight from the U.K. press. I was able to focus on a purpose larger than myself, to be wearing the same uniform as everybody else, to feel normal for the first time in my life. And accomplish some of the biggest challenges that I ever had. You know, I was training to become an Apache helicopter pilot. You don't get a pass for being a prince.*

I was a really good candidate for the military. I was a young man in my 20s suffering from shock. But I was now in the front seat of an Apache shooting it, flying it, monitoring four radios simultaneously and being there to save and help anybody that was on the ground with a radio screaming, "We need support, we need air support." That was my calling. I felt healing from that weirdly.

It felt like I was turning pain into a purpose. I didn't have the awareness at the time that I was living my life in adrenaline, and that was the case from age 12, from the moment that I was told that my mom had died. The war for me unknowingly was when my mum died.[194]

Harry stated in a separate interview that his military career allowed him to hide away from the media focus and to no longer be treated differently from others. Therefore, changing his environment and separation from life as a royal for ten years, seems to have been a significant factor in stabilising and managing his PTSI symptoms. His former girlfriends both commented on his Jekyll-and-Hyde existence. Harry was happy when he was away from prying eyes and publicity and 'tightly wound up' when he was in London (p.280). It seems what they were experiencing was the difference between Harry's calm, happy, stable mindset away from the public

---

[194] (Cooper, 2023)

gaze, compared with Harry's hyperarousal in the hostile environment of the urban jungle, surrounded by paparazzi and cameras. This fact further supports the theory that Harry wanted to escape the monarchy and change his environment. Harry left the military in 2015. He had enjoyed ten years of stability. He struggled with a transition back into royal life and admits he wasn't sure he knew how to be a Royal. Approximately one year later, Harry met Meghan and it seems he clung to her as a potential escape route – to find that same stability in a kindred spirit and away from the UK.

Harry stated he found spirituality and healing in nature. A kind of 'mindfulness' in the moment. During an expedition to the South Pole, *"the silence was holy. [He was] overcome with joy. Months and months of anxiety passed away* "(p.254). This speaks volumes, to the healing power of changing one's environment and the people one spends time with.

Harry stated the age of 28-32 years *"was a nightmare time in his life."* Meghan Markle encouraged Harry to seek help through therapy when they met, because of his anger. Harry knew this was essential for his relationship with Meghan to work.[195]

One of the most difficult issues for Harry is having compassion for others when his own life is hard and feelings of helplessness cause him significant anxiety.[196] This is perhaps evident in his TV and media interviews, and his memoir 'Spare.'

In his interview *"Harry admits he smoked pot and used cocaine. And he writes that in his late 20s he felt "hopeless" and "lost." He sought out help from a therapist for the first time seven years ago. And he reveals he's also tried more experimental treatments, [Including] psychedelics, Ayahuasca, psilocybin, mushrooms."* Harry stated, *"I would never recommend people to do this recreationally.*

---

[195] (Mountbatten-Windsor, 2021)
[196] (Today, 2022)

But doing it with the right people if you are suffering from a huge amount of loss, grief or trauma, then these things have a way of working as a medicine. Harry says he's used psychedelics to help cope with grief.[197] He advocates the use of psychedelics in conjunction with therapy and under the supervision of a clinician. He stated their use helped him to *"let go of rigid pre-concepts"* (p.255). Rigid perceptions are synonymous with MI and PB. For example, cynicism, suspiciousness and a one-dimensional viewpoint. The ability to reflect on multiple perspectives on any given situation requires Emotional Intelligence and empathy, which in turn protects against the development of MI and PB.[198]

Helping others, such as through the Invictus Games or charitable projects in Africa were also remedial (p.255). The act of assisting others less fortunate, shifts one from a state of being self-

---

[197] (Cooper, 2023)
[198] (Carter, 2020)

absorbed in one's own suffering and to look outward to the suffering of others – to gain perspective.[199]

Harry joined forces with Oprah Winfrey and other celebrities on a mental health project called 'The me you can't see.' He stated *"all over the world people are in some kind of mental, emotional, psychological pain [and] carrying around some form of unresolved grief, trauma or loss. We should be focused on the things that feed our soul and just as much as that diet of what we put into our bellies, it's the same with the diet that we put into our brains – what we read, what we consume. One thing I've learned is that sharing your story in order to be able to save a life or help others is absolutely critical. I see it as a responsibility that rests on our shoulders, especially if we have a platform or if we have any form of influence."*[200] However, Harry's behaviour suggests his own recovery is not yet complete. This may not be the

---

[199] (Carter, 2020)
[200] (ET-Canada, 2021)

best time for Harry to be advising others on their mental health journey.

Harry stated, wearing a beard helped him feel calmer, though he could not explain why (p.331). He questioned whether it was a security blanket or a mask. He had found articles on the phenomenon. Perhaps Harry did not like to see his boyish looks in the mirror – a constant reminder to a difficult period during his youth. The beard providing a new, adult identity – a mirror image he could feel comfortable with – a reinvented Harry.

Hopefully, as a husband and father, living on his own terms away from the UK and royal duties - Harry will finally heal, become more compassionate towards the family that raised him with love and empathy and find an internal sense of peace. At this time Harry states he is happy and with his family in California. However, his words and actions (to a greater extent) are contrary to his behaviour at this time.

213

The Press - the other side of the story

The Princes and the Press, a two-part documentary, aired on BBC two in November 2021.[201] Journalist Amol Rajan interviews Royal correspondents and journalists, including those working for the BBC and the tabloid press. Episode one begins with a soundbite from Harry, stating he is acutely aware of how scared his family are of the Press turning on them. He will not be bullied into playing the game that killed his mum. It was suggested that Prince William and Prince Harry tried to control their hatred of the media, by controlling the media. However, the media is not controllable.

Suing the press is likely to result in unflattering news coverage, whereas if the Royals 'play the game,' the tabloid press will be favourable.

---

[201] (Rajan, 2021)

William is playing the game and engaging with the Press. Harry is purposefully uncooperative – such as, turning away from the cameras and scowling. The programme stated there is a significant degree of manipulation of the Press from the Royal courts, which echoes Harry's assertions.

The programme is interested in how and why narratives relating to the Royal family emerge. For example, accusations that Prince William was work-shy manifested because the Press began questioning why he was not visible and only had two royal engagements in a particular year. This seemed to be a way of goading Prince William to show himself – a reminder that he was not fulfilling his obligation to the public (or the Press). Prince William understands he will be King one day and press coverage of his journey towards becoming Monarch will be a matter of record. Therefore, the nature of the coverage is important. He seems to now be working in cooperation with the Press to this end.

Harry however, seems to have nothing to lose from being obstructive and suing the Press.

According to the documentary - a Private investigator (PI), worked for News of the World commencing early 2000. The motive for using a PI to gather information on Prince Harry, was his popularity and ability to sell more newspapers than Prince William. It was stated, there was a lot of voicemail hacking on Harry's girlfriend Chelsy. They looked into her medical records. Had she had an abortion, any sexual diseases, ex-boyfriends? The PI stated, his actions were ruthless because he was greedy and taking cocaine. He was living in a fake state of grandeur. He feels bad for being a party to robbing Harry of his teenage years. He was part of the phone hacking scandal - using illegal and unethical methods to get stories on Prince Harry between the 90's and 2011. The position of News Group newspapers is that they don't accept this was happening at the Sun newspaper and there was only limited use of these methods at the News of the World. The princes wanted to reach a resolution with the Press. At some stage Harry decided to continue pursuing the issue. Harry wanted to talk openly about the hacking. William has come to realise it may not be in his best interests to push the issue.

According to another PI interviewed by Rajan for the programme, the Press hired him in the US to obtain information on Meghan, her family and ex-boyfriends. The PI stated, re-selling data to the media is illegal and against the rules. He admits to knowingly participating in this illegal activity.

Despite the Royal family's motto 'never complain, never explain,' it was extraordinary to receive a press statement from Harry in 2016, stating - A line has been crossed. Meghan has been exposed to a wave of abuse, racial undertones and sexism. This statement coincided with Prince Charles' tour in the Middle East and therefore, took the limelight away from his father – whose publicity should have taken priority, as per protocol. One potential reason for this type of misstep is that every principal Royal has their own 'house' and press team. For example, Queen Elizabeth II – Buckingham Palace, Prince Charles and Camilla – Clarence House, the Duke and Duchess of Cambridge and Prince Harry – Kensington Palace. These separate houses did not always work in tandem with each other, resulting in a breakdown in communication and a competitiveness over coverage. In the months following Prince Harry's statement, Meghan's press coverage reached its most positive level.

The Press coverage of the Duke and Duchess' wedding was flattering. Meghan was described as a beautiful bride and the press stated it was a breath of fresh air to have a new addition to the family who is biracial.

However, within days of the wedding, the Press sensed things weren't as happy as they had been before Harry and Meghan had wed.

For example, there were complaints about the way Meghan was treating staff and tension between the Princes William and Harry, Meghan and Kate – and between Harry and Meghan with the royal household.

Andrew Marr draws parallels between the Royal family and the nature of politics – presenting one image to the outside world, while another remains behind the scenes. He stated politicians have long envied the united face of the Monarchy, but as soon as that cracks, there is a way in for the Press to get a story.

Johnny Dymond, BBC Royal correspondent stated, Harry has a visceral reaction to the media, to notebooks and cameras. This statement of fact correlates with Harry's own account of his posttraumatic symptoms.

Dan Wootton (formerly of the Sun newspaper) stated the negative stories regarding the strife in the Royal household remained unpublished in British newspapers. No one wanted to be the first to break the news, which was eventually exposed after six months. The first story that was run by the Sun in 2018 involved the tiara Meghan wore for her wedding. She wanted to wear a particular tiara with an emerald but was refused due to the historical significance of the jewellery. Harry allegedly stated "what Meghan wants, Meghan gets" implying Meghan's demanding nature and that she was 'being difficult.' Queen Elizabeth II reportedly spoke to Harry, either in relation to his behaviour or warning him of Meghan's attitude.

Peter Hunt, BBC Royal Correspondent stated issues arose as a result of the fracturing of the relationship between Prince William and Harry. News stories were being leaked by employed and former staff within the Royal households. This statement reinforces Harry's own belief this was happening.

A lawyer representing the Duchess of Sussex was interviewed with Meghan's permission. She stated the Press story that a personal assistant working for Harry and Meghan resigned due to Meghan's unpleasant treatment of her, was not true. The Royal household did not support Meghan with a statement of rebuttal regarding these allegations at the time. However, Clarence House and Kensington Palace released a joint statement for the documentary stating, *"A free, responsible and open press is of vital importance to a healthy democracy. However, too often overblown and unfounded claims from unnamed sources are presented as facts and it is disappointing when anyone, including the BBC gives them credibility."* Rajan, concludes that Royal journalism is subjective.

Holding the Press accountable

'Cancel culture' in today's society - is where free speech and opinion, perceived as offensive, results in the cold-shoulder treatment and ostracizing the publisher of the comments - attempting to wipe out their existence, their importance and even their good work and achievements. Society is attempting to control language, narratives and perceptions. However, this behaviour is coming under criticism for prohibiting free speech, debate and critical thinking, as well as attempts to rewrite or eradicate some events in history. It is important to consider that society may influence Harry and Meghan's perceptions and behaviours as a couple keen to be relevant and relatable to their fan base.

What must be encouraging for Meghan and Harry, is that the public are actively challenging the Press too - in their droves. That said, free speech must not be cancelled, where it does not incite hatred or violence (for example). It is okay to disagree respectfully with someone else's opinion. Harry and Meghan have been widely criticised for trying to cancel, terminate the employment of, or open a case of litigation against anyone whose comments and opinions offend them. It seems the more they try and control the Press and media, the more they open themselves to ridicule and scrutiny.

Taking on the Press through litigation is not exclusive to Harry and Meghan. Other complainants have already had success in addressing the phone hacking scandal involving News International journalists. The paper News of the World was disbanded in 2011. The trial was reported to cost up to £100 million. Former News of the World editor, Andy Coulson was convicted and the trial prompted change to the regulation of the Press. The scandal involved celebrities, public figures and victims of crime. Phone hacking was used to access phone voicemail to obtain information that could be used to create news for the tabloid press. Five journalists and private investigators and editors pleaded guilty before the trial began.[202] Relatives of deceased British soldiers, and victims of the 7th of July 2005 London bombings had also been hacked. Directors, executives, legal advisors and senior police chiefs resigned from their positions.[203]

Following the Leveson inquiry into the Press Complaints Commission and the phone hacking scandal, Queen Elizabeth II set her seal on the Royal Charter for self-regulation of the Press in 2013. The Charter comes under two Acts of Parliament, the Crime and Courts Act 2013 and the Enterprise and Regulatory Reform Act 2013. The development of the Press Recognition Panel (PRP), which is a corporation involved with the recognition of press regulators in the UK, soon followed the Charter. One such regulator began in October 2016 called IMPRESS (Independent Monitor for the Press), which became the UK's

---

[202] (BBC, 2014)
[203] (Wiki, 2023)

first approved press regulator. IMPRESS is fully compliant with the Leveson inquiry recommendations, unlike some other regulatory bodies. IMPRESS regulates over 200 publications at this time. However, none of the titles are national newspapers, who have opted to use their own regulator, which largely complies with the recommendations made in the Leveson inquiry report. IMPRESS acts against various forms of publication, including social media and blog posts. *"On 26 March 2019, IMPRESS was reconfirmed as the UK's approved, independent press regulator by the Press Recognition Panel (PRP). The PRP clarified that "This means that, amongst other things, IMPRESS is independent of the print and online publishers it regulates, is appropriately funded, and has systems in place to protect the public."*[204]

---

[204] (Wiki, 2023)

There has been victory. The Press have been exposed and shamed for abhorrent and inexcusable working practices. High profile individuals have lost their jobs, their reputations and some lost their liberty (incarcerated in Her Majesty's prisons). Many have convictions. Their names and faces have been indelibly paraded for the world to see. [205] Through social action and with the support of each other, victims have succeeded in holding the Press accountable, not just for past actions, but also future behaviour.

The regulators are now in place to hold the Press to account, as well as other forms of media and publishing. Harry's Grandmother, Queen Elizabeth II supported and approved the legislation governing the Royal charter for the self-regulation of the Press. Yet Harry maintains the monarchy have not helped him and Meghan.

---

[205] (BBC, 2014)

IPSO, which is also a Press regulator is "*launching an investigation based on complaints from two women's charities - the Fawcett Society and the Wilde Foundation,*" regarding an opinion piece written for the Sun newspaper by TV personality Jeremy Clarkson. In the article he stated "*he hoped Prince Harry's wife Meghan would one day be forced to parade naked through the streets.*" IPSO has "*now received more than 25,100 complaints from members of the public*" relating to this article. The Sun withdrew the piece and published an apology.[206]

So too, did Presenter Piers Morgan leave his role on Good Morning Britain after "*Ofcom said it was investigating his comments after receiving 41,000 complaints*" regarding his comments about Meghan's mental health claims. Meghan chose to make complaints directly to the broadcasters, rather than through regulating bodies.[207]

---

[206] (Ravikumar, 2023)
[207] (BBC, 2021)

Harry, Meghan and members of the Royal family are afforded greater protections from the media since the traumatic accident and death of Princess Diana. IPSO *"added the following clause to its policies as a means of preventing future paparazzi-provoked accidents: "i) Journalists must not engage in intimidation, harassment, or persistent pursuit. ii) They must not persist in questioning, telephoning, pursuing, or photographing individuals once asked to desist; nor remain on their property when asked to leave and must not follow them. If requested, they must identify themselves and whom they represent."*[208]

Following the incident involving Diana and the Paparazzi, California passed legislation in 1998, known as Civil Code 1708.8. Photographers trespassing on private property are breaching this law. In 2011, the state of California went further and introduced the Vehicle Code Section 40008. This criminal code states *"if you interfered*

---

[208] (Pajer, 2017)

with a driver and you follow too closely, you make it difficult for them to drive, you act recklessly because you are trying to capture an image or a recording for a commercial purpose, you have committed a misdemeanour."[209]

The Guardian paper published an article regarding Kate Middleton and the issue of privacy in 2007. Stating, *"While there may be an eerie similarity between the press harassment Ms Middleton is being subjected to and that which faced the young Princess Diana, the legal landscape relating to such harassment has seen a significant shift. This shift towards greater privacy protection has been upheld in recent cases such as, Prince of Wales v Associated Newspapers (Charles's journal case)."*[210]

Where the press publishes photographs that breach her privacy then she can go to court but, by this stage, that which was private will have been

---

[209] (Pajer, 2017)
[210] (Forbes, 2007)

made very public. She could apply to the court for an injunction preventing publication of pictures taken of her going about her private business but while she may be able to provide grounds for such an order it would be difficult to secure an open-ended one covering all media. Even if she were to secure protection against some or all of the UK press, this will do little to keep foreign paparazzi and publications at bay. Consumer demand will always ensure there is a price for her picture, the best she can hope for is to use the law to level the playing field on home ground.[211] This evidence supports the fact that the Royal family were correct in advising Harry and Meghan to try and ignore the Press and accept they cannot control everything published. Furthermore, that other family members have faced their own battles with the media and have tried to support the Duke and Duchess with the reality of their situation.

---

[211] (Forbes, 2007)

The Guardian published an article in 2006 titled, 'Charles claims victory in Hong Kong diary case' regarding his legal battle against Associated Newspapers (including the Mail on Sunday) for publishing his private journals. *"The 3,000-word journal, handwritten by the prince on his way back from the Hong Kong handover nearly nine years ago under the heading "The Great Chinese Takeaway", was one of eight such reports written after foreign trips in the 1990s that were passed to the newspaper by a disaffected former secretary in the prince's office. Copies of the journals had been circulated privately to the prince's friends. Charles saw himself as a political "dissident" because of the views he expressed in letters to ministers."*[212] Just as Meghan's private correspondence with her father was leaked to the Press, so too has King Charles III had his own experience of this. Harry may perceive himself to be on a lifetime mission to reform the media and the Press. However, he is in no way single-handedly achieving great reform.

---

[212] (Bates, 2006)

He is not the first Royal or celebrity to take the Press to task through litigation. The phone hacking scandal was a landmark case, which many claimants collaborated on and achieved success. His mother's tragic death was also a catalyst for changes in law.

Conclusion

The Harry and Meghan story will continue long after the publication of this book. How they decide to approach the future is not yet known. They will undoubtedly understand that public sympathy for them and their popularity has significantly waned. Their 'brand,' their reputation and credibility has been damaged by the release of their docuseries, Harry's memoir and their version of the truth, which seems to be flawed. They have perhaps portrayed themselves as untrustworthy, unreliable sources of information and self-serving.

Their relationships with family have been damaged. Harry and Meghan have isolated themselves from their kin and caused their relations harm. The first rule of telling your story to help people on their healing journey, is that you avoid causing injury to others in the process. Otherwise, you become just as culpable as the people you blame. This research suggests Harry and Meghan have perpetrated Moral Injury by betraying people who trusted them and by risking the reputations and livelihoods of the monarchy.

Their mental health has been damaged. Harry and Meghan seem to have been affected by Moral Injury too and this has led to Posttraumatic Blame – regardless of whether their perception of injustice or injury is rational or distorted.

Harry describes himself as suffering PTSI, anxiety, agoraphobia, panic attacks and phobic reactions to cameras, London and the UK. His mental health issues are longstanding, since the age of twelve. He was able to avoid the Press to a large extent during his school years and during military service, but his unresolved grief and Moral Injury at the traumatic death of his mother is something unavoidable and with him wherever he goes.

Regardless of anything Harry and Meghan might say to the contrary – research suggests they were always going to leave the UK and the monarchy.

There is nothing the Royal family could do or say that would alleviate their discomfort, or encourage them to stay, because the situation was untenable for them. Meghan could not tolerate the environment, nor sacrifice her values to stay. Trying to be 'something she's not' was unsustainable and causing her psychological distress.

Unfortunately, it seems people were unable to see the best in Meghan because the persistent stress she experienced affected the presentation of her behaviour. Sadly, it seems Harry has caused his wife vicarious trauma and distorted her perception of danger. He is convinced she is going to die as a consequence of the Press. Therefore, Meghan's husband controlled the narrative she was fed, he prevented her from becoming a successful Royal and to shine confidently in her new role. This seems to have contributed significantly to difficulties with her mental health. In any event, it is probably fair to say Meghan was never suited to life as a princess or a Duchess. The reality was not what she expected and her character is not befitting a senior Royal. For example, her values of independence, autonomy and freedom of speech (opinion).

It seems Meghan believed marrying a prince would catapult her public profile to exulted heights and that she would have the power to control the institution and public opinion about her. She stated her archetypal princess would be She-Ra, the powerful, sword wielding, royal rebel. It seems Meghan got more than she bargained for. Her expectations were not met. Instead of controlling the situation, it seems Harry has controlled Meghan.

This research determined that Harry and Meghan have perhaps both been naïve in their assumptions of the monarchy, what to expect and their place within the institution. The monarchy's failure to meet their expectations has led to MI and PB. There is an overall sense that the Duke and Duchess feel 'entitled' – entitled to shape the monarchy in their own image, entitled to round the clock protection, entitled to royal titles for their children, entitled to control the opinions of others and entitled to apologies and accountability from senior royals.

Harry appears to be driven by a powerful need to avoid a royal life under the microscope and camera lens. He was unfamiliar with performing a full-time role as a Royal and unsure if this was the right path for him. Long before meeting Meghan Markle, he longed for privacy, normality and freedom from the monarchy. Meghan facilitated his exit from the UK, the institution and his obligations.

If they had a checklist of qualities they were looking for in a partner, it would not be surprising if Harry's list included, free-spirited, entrepreneurial, maternal, confident, powerful, head-strong or strong willed, ambitious, humorous, energetic, adventurous, foreign and someone 'with a plan.'

Meghan's checklist of qualities in a partner could possibly be someone who would appreciate her power as a woman and her ability to achieve and succeed. A man who would be willing to put her and her needs first (always). A partner who would support her unconditionally in all her ambitions. She may have also sought a partner with significant status (even though she has disputed this). Someone who could raise her profile. It seems she was also pursuing her childhood fantasy of marrying a prince and being a princess.

In conclusion, Harry and Meghan are not at fault for wanting to meet their own needs through their marriage to each other. Neither Meghan or Harry was compatible with a royal life. Their decision to leave the monarchy and the UK was appropriate for their health and wellbeing.

A wonderful outcome would be if Harry and Meghan were honest about the difficulties caused by Harry's symptoms of psychological injury, which made it impossible to stay in the UK, and

Meghan's inability to cope with the restrictions of Royal life without blaming others for their decision to leave. There is no bogeyman. The issues lie with them and no one else.

Both Harry and Meghan have experienced difficulties with their mental health. Harry's psychological injury predates their relationship and began after the death of his mother when he was twelve years of age. Meghan's psychological injury seems to have developed soon after their relationship became public, following a difficult transition into the monarchy after their marriage and during pregnancy. It seems much of her distress may be due to Harry's behaviour, his anger and his distorted perception of danger.

There is significant evidence in this case study to demonstrate Harry is affected by symptoms associated with Moral Injury, Posttraumatic Blame and PTSD - including personality traits of querulousness, grandeur, projecting his own personality on to others, distorted perceptions, embitterment, rigid perceptions, low emotional intelligence and desire for revenge.

Harry's case study of Moral Injury and Posttraumatic Blame, are demonstrative of why it is important to empathise with the struggles of affected individuals and to understand their need to hold on to the past.

"Hold on to the past and what happened if you feel you must, just make sure you turn the experience into wisdom, not bitterness. The goal is not to let go, move on or forgive – the aim is to understand, learn, grow in wisdom, teach, safeguard self and others" (Claire Carter, 2022)

Harry appears to desire recovery and healing from his trauma, yet perhaps reluctant to let go of his pain and injury. Rumination (which keeps his wounds open) and anger, seems to be a necessary fuel for him to function. Sadly, this could see him experience even more loss, in pursuit of the justice, revenge and vindication he seeks.

REFERENCES

60-minutes-Australia. (2022, July 31). *The Trouble with Meghan*. Retrieved from YouTube: https://www.youtube.com/watch?v=uFrcx3l_n r4

Aljazeera. (2022, April 3). *Jordan's Prince Hamzah bin Hussein renounces his title*. Retrieved from Aljazeera: https://www.aljazeera.com/news/2022/4/3/j ordans-prince-hamzah-bin-hussein-renounces-his-title

American-Psychiatric-Association. (2020). *DSM-5 Factsheets, Changes in PTSD Criteria*. Retrieved from https://www.psychiatry.org/File%20Library/P sychiatrists/Practice/DSM/APA_DSM-5-PTSD.pdf

Balakrishnan, A. (2008, April 7). *The press pack that chased Diana*. Retrieved from The Guardian: https://amp.theguardian.com/uk/2008/apr/0 7/paparazzi

Barnes, H., Hurley, R., & Taber, K. (2019, April 23). *Moral Injury and PTSD: Often Co-Occuring Yet Mechanistically Different*. Retrieved from The Journal of NeuroPsychiatry and Clinical Neurosciences:

https://neuro.psychiatryonline.org/doi/10.117
6

Bates, S. (2006, March 18). *Charles claims victory in Hong Kong diary case*. Retrieved from The Guardian: https://www.theguardian.com/media/2006/mar/18/mailonsunday.associatednewspapers

Batty, D. (2007, November 14). *Ambulance driver defends slow Diana journey*. Retrieved from The Guardian: https://www.theguardian.com/uk/2007/nov/14/monarchy.davidbatty

BBC. (2014, June 25). *Phone-hacking trial explained*. Retrieved from BBC News: https://www.bbc.co.uk/news/uk-24894403

BBC. (2021, March 10). *Meghan and Harry interview: Palace taking race issues 'very seriously'*. Retrieved from BBC News: https://www.bbc.co.uk/news/uk-56340451

BBC. (2021, March 10). *Piers Morgan leaves ITV's Good Morning Britain after row over Meghan remarks*. Retrieved from BBC News: https://www.bbc.co.uk/news/entertainment-arts-56334082

BBC-News. (2021, December 2). *Meghan wins ruling in Mail on Sunday privacy fight*. Retrieved from

BBC News: https://www.bbc.co.uk/news/uk-59502787

Bedigan, M. (2022, December 7). *Harry and Meghan accept Ripple of Hope Award for racial justice work: 'A ripple of hope can turn into a wave of change'*. Retrieved from Independent: https://www.independent.co.uk/life-style/royal-family/harry-meghan-robert-kennedy-awards-b2240365.html

Bessel-Van-Der-kalk. (2015). *The Body Keeps the Score: Mind, Brain and Body in the Transformation of Trauma.* Penguin.

Braddick, I., & Micallef, C. (2022, September 18). *ROYAL BLOOD Why do Prince Edward's children not have official prince and princess titles?* Retrieved from The Sun: https://www.thesun.co.uk/news/14292805/prince-edward-children-louise-james-official-titles/amp/

Calado, B., Luke, T., Deborah, C., Landstrom, S., & Otgaar, H. (2021, September 27). *Implanting false autobiographical memories for repeated events.* Retrieved from Taylor and Francis Online: https://www.tandfonline.com/doi/full/10.1080/09658211.2021.1981944

Campbell, S. (2022, September 9). *Camilla, the new Queen Consort.* Retrieved from BBC News: https://www.bbc.co.uk/news/uk-59150068

Carter, C. (2020). *Overwhelming Injustice and Posttraumatic Blame Theory.* International: Amazon.

Carter, C. (2021, September). *Organisational injustice in UK frontline services and onset of Moral Injury, Post Traumatic Embitterment Disorder (PTED) and PTSD.* Retrieved from International Journal of Law, Crime and Justice: https://doi.org/10.1016/j.ijlcj.2021.100483

Colbert, S. (2023, January 10). *Prince Harry, The Duke of Sussex Talks #Spare with Stephen Colbert - EXTENDED INTERVIEW.* Retrieved from YouTube: https://www.youtube.com/watch?v=E6l0ObY2XVM

Cooper, A. (2023, January 8). *Prince Harry: The 60 Minutes Interview Transcript.* Retrieved from https://www.cbsnews.com/news/prince-harry-interview-transcript-60-minutes-2023-01-08/

Coughlan, S. (2021, November 10). *Duchess of Sussex weighed up calling father 'daddy'.* Retrieved

from BBC News:
https://www.bbc.co.uk/news/uk-59236643

Crawford-Smith. (2023, February 15). *Mehan Markle's 'Endless Conversations About Kate' Past Comment Resurfaces.* Retrieved from Newsweek: http://www.newsweek.com/what-meghan-markle-said-kate-middleton-prince-harry-blog-post-1781445

Deprince, A. (2001). *Trauma and Posttraumatic Responses: An Examination of Fear and Betrayal.* Retrieved from ResearchGate: https://www.researchgate.net/publication/34280779_trauma_and_posttraumatic_responses_an_examination_of_fear_and_betrayal

Donlevy, K. (2023, February 5). *Samantha Markle serves court papers to royals in defamation suit against Harry and Meghan.* Retrieved from New York Post: https://nypost.com/2023/02/05/prince-harry-served-in-samantha-markle-suit-against-meghan/

Duell, M. (2021, March 10). *All the WORKING Royals who don't get full protection demanded by Harry and Meghan: Members of The Firm like Princess Anne, Prince Edward and Sophie Wessex don't have 24/7 security despite hundreds of engagements a year.* Retrieved from Mail Online: https://www.dailymail.co.uk/news/article-

9346083/Meghan-Markle-interview-Members-Royal-Family-dont-police-protection.html

Duell, M. (2022, April 21). *Read Prince Harry's bombshell US TV interview in full: Every word so far from royal's sit down with NBC's Hoda Kotb including his thoughts on the Queen, his life in the US and William and Charles.* Retrieved from Mail Online: https://www.dailymail.co.uk/news/article-10735723/Full-transcript-Prince-Harrys-TV-interview-NBCs-Today.html

Duncan, P. (2020, January 18). *Meghan gets twice as many negative headlines as positive, analysis finds.* Retrieved from The Guardian: https://www.theguardian.com/global/2020/jan/18/meghan-gets-more-than-twice-as-many-negative-headlines-as-positive

ET-Canada. (2021, May 2021). *Prince Harry Opens Up About What Triggers His Anxiety.* Retrieved from YouTube: https://youtu.be/B-jAwGMutLA

Ferguson, E. (2023, February 13). *Prince Harry and Meghan to stop dishing dirt on Royal Family in new Sussex rebrand.* Retrieved from Express: https://www.express.co.uk/news/royal/1733206/prince-harry-meghan-markle-news-sussex-rebrand-royal-family/amp

Forbes, E. (2007, January 10). *Can you stop the paparazzi?* Retrieved from The Guardian: https://www.theguardian.com/media/2007/jan/10/privacy.royalsandthemedia

Foussianes, C. (2020, June 8). *Meghan Markle and Prince Harry Are Holding Meetings About Black Lives Matter and How They Can Help.* Retrieved from Town and Country: https://www.townandcountrymag.com/society/tradition/a32800942/meghan-markle-prince-harry-black-lives-matter-meetings/

Freyd, J. (2019). *What is Betrayal Trauma Theory?* Retrieved from University of Oregon: https://dynamic.uoregon.edu/jjf/defineBT.html

Freyd, J., & Smith, C. (2013). *Institutional Betrayal.* Retrieved from University of Oregon: https://dynamic.uoregon.edu/jjf/articles/sfinpress.pdf

Galpin, K. (2023, February 15). *eghan wrote about 'Princess wedding' and dreams of being 'royal rebel' before meeting Harry.* Retrieved from OK: https://www.ok.co.uk/royal/kate-middleton-meghan-markle-blog-29225375

GMA. (2023, January 9). *Prince Harry on what led to royal rift, what he thins is needed for*

reconciliation. Retrieved from You Tube:
https://youtu.be/2u6dxjykCFk

Gov.uk. (2023, February 21). *Peerage Act 1963*.
Retrieved from Legislation.gov.uk:
https://www.legislation.gov.uk/ukpga/1963/4
8

Grierson, J. (2020, October 11). *Meghan: 'I'm told I was
the most trolled person in the world'*. Retrieved
from The Guardian:
https://www.theguardian.com/uk-
news/2020/oct/11/meghan-im-told-i-was-the-
most-trolled-person-in-the-world

Herman, J. (1997). *Trauma and Recovery: The Aftermath
of Violence - From Domestic Abuse to Political
Terror.* New York: Basic Books.

Hills, M. (2018, August 16). *Meghan Markle name-
dropped Kate Middleton and a 'childhood
fantasy' of being a princess in a super old blog
post.* Retrieved from Marie Claire:
https://www.marieclaire.co.uk/news/celebrity
-news/meghan-markle-the-tig-blog-post-
611897

Hoffman, J. (2022, January 16). *Prince Harry to Britain:
This Is What I Need to Keep My Family Safe.*
Retrieved from Vanity Fair:

https://www.vanityfair.com/style/2017/09/m
eghan-markle-cover-story

Ibrahim, S. (2022, October 27). *Prince Harry reveals how much he was paid for memoir — and where money will go.* Retrieved from New York Post: https://nypost.com/2022/10/27/prince-harry-reveals-how-much-he-was-paid-for-memoir-where-money-will-go/

ITV-News. (2023, January 6). *Senior Taliban leader hits out at Prince Harry's claims he killed 25 people in Afghanistan.* Retrieved from ITV News: itv.com/news.2023-01-06/senior-taliban-leader-hits-out-at-harrys-claim-he-killed-25-in-afghanistan

James, L. (2023, January 13). *Prince Harry says he cut bombshells from book as royals would 'never forgive' him.* Retrieved from Independent: https://www.independent.co.uk/life-style/royal-family/prince-harry-new-book-spare-royal-family-b2261907.html

Jenkins, L. (2023, February 1). *Remembering Our Past: What Are the Factors That Can Affect Autobiographical Memory?* Retrieved from Psychreg: https://www.psychreg.org/factors-autobiographical-memory/

Jordan, A., & Litz, B. (2014). *Prolonged Greif Disorder: Diagnostic Assessment and Treatment.* Retrieved from American Psychological Association: http://www.apa.ort/pubs/journals/features/pro-a0036836.pdf

Kashner, S. (2017, October). *Meghan Markle, Wild About Harry!* Retrieved from Vanity Fair: https://www.vanityfair.com/style/2017/09/meghan-markle-cover-story

Kato, B. (2022, December 8). *Here's how much Netflix paid Prince Harry, Meghan Markle for documentary.* Retrieved from New York Post: https://nypost.com/2022/12/08/how-much-did-netflix-pay-prince-harry-meghan-markle-for-documentary/

Koenig, H. (2019, June 28). *Assessment of Moral Injury in Veterans and Active Duty Military Personnel with PTSD: A Review.* Retrieved from Frontiers in Psychology: https://www.frontiersin.org/articles/10.3389/fpsyt.2019.00443/full

Lester, G., Wilson, B., Griffin, L., & Mullen, P. (2004). Unusually persistent complainants. *British Journal of Psychiatry*, 352-356. Retrieved from British Journal of Psychiatry.

Linden, M., & Maercker, A. (2011). *Embitterment - Societal, psychological, and clinical perspectives.* New York: Springer Wien.

Linden, M., & Maercker, A. (2011). *Embitterment: Societal, psychological, and clinical perspectives.* New York: Springer Science and Business Media.

Linden, M., Rotter, M., & Schippan, B. (2007, February). *The psychopathology of posttraumatic embitterment disorders.* Retrieved from NCBI PubMed: http://www.ncbi.nlm.nig.gov/pubmed/173180 08

Litz, B., Lebowitz, L., Gray, M., & Nash, W. (2016). *Adaptive Disclosure: A New Treatment for Military Trauma, Loss and Moral Injury.* New York: Guildford Press.

Markle. (2014, July 7). *Tig Talk with Princess Alia Al-Senussi.* Retrieved from The Tig: http://web.archive.org/web/20150403184128 /http:/thetig.com/tig-talk-princess-alia-al-senussi/

Markle, M. (2021, March 8). *MARK MY WORDS Meghan Markle Oprah interview: read the full transcript of Duchess and Prince Harry's bombshell confessions.* Retrieved from The Sun:

https://www.thesun.co.uk/news/14277841/m
eghan-markle-oprah-interview-full-transcript/

McDowell, E. (2022, December 1). *The first trailer for Meghan Markle and Prince Harry's Netflix documentary is here. Here's a complete timeline of their relationship.* Retrieved from Insider: https://www.insider.com/prince-harry-meghan-markle-relationship-timeline

Miller, F. (2021, August 16). *When was Prince Harry in Afghanistan? Inside the royal's fight against the Taliban.* Retrieved from Express: https://www.express.co.uk/news/royal/14775 67/when-was-prince-harry-in-afghanistan-fight-taliban-evg

Mills, S. (2022, May 24). *Does the Commonwealth have a future after Queen Elizabeth?* Retrieved from Reuters: https://www.reuters.com/world/does-commonwealth-have-future-after-queen-elizabeth-2022-05-23/

Mohan-Hickson, M. (2023, January 8). *Prince Harry Interview: full transcript of Duke of Sussex ITV programme with Tom Bradby - read every word.* Retrieved from Bristol World: https://www.bristolworld.com/culture/televisi on/prince-harry-interview-full-transcript-of-

duke-of-sussex-itv-programme-with-tom-
bradby-3978749

Moody, M. (2022, November 22). *Inside Princess Diana's
Complicated Friendship with Sarah Ferguson,
Duchess of York.* Retrieved from Town and
Country:
https://www.townandcountrymag.com/society
/tradition/a22482954/princess-diana-sarah-
ferguson-duchess-of-york-relationship/

Moore, M. (2023, January 27). *How Prince Harry plans to
spend the proceeds from his memoir.* Retrieved
from Hello:
https://www.hellomagazine.com/royalty/2022
1027155404/prince-harry-charity-donations-
from-spare-proceeds/

Morgan, C. (2020, July 6). *Prince Charles plans to
'dampen a sense of entitlement' to housing and
other perks among minor members of The Firm
as he prepares to become king, royal author
claims.* Retrieved from Mail Online:
https://www.dailymail.co.uk/femail/article-
8494561/Prince-Charles-plans-dampen-sense-
entitlement-royals-royal-author-claims.html

Morris, J., & Smith, M. (2023, January 12). *Prince Harry's
popularity falls further as 'Spare' hits the shelves.*
Retrieved from YouGov:
https://yougov.co.uk/topics/politics/articles-

reports/2023/01/12/prince-harrys-
popularity-falls-further-spare-hits-

Morris, S. (2021, March 9). *Prince Archie? Why Meghan
Markle and Prince Harry's Son Does Not Have
Royal Title*. Retrieved from Newsweek:
https://www.newsweek.com

Mountbatten-Windsor, H. (2021, May 21). *Prince
Harry's Shocking Mental Health Struggles
Revealed In 'The Me You Can't See'*. Retrieved
from YouTube: https://youtu.be/XOgGU-
PRGpU

Mountbatten-Windsor, H. (2023). *Spare*. London:
Penguin Random House.

Nanan-Sen, S. (2023, March 23). *Prince Harry walks into
photographer as he arrives at High Court for
legal battle*. Retrieved from GB News:
https://www.gbnews.com/royal/prince-harry-
arrives-at-the-royal-courts-of-justice-as-duke-
of-sussex-set-for-another-legal-battle

Pajer, N. (2017, August 31). *How paparazzi laws have
changed since Princess Diana's death*. Retrieved
from Yahoo News:
https://uk.news.yahoo.com/paparazzi-laws-
changed-since-princess-dianas-death-
001001650.html

PA-Reporters. (2021, March 30). *Archbishop of Canterbury: Harry and Meghan's legal wedding was on the Saturday.* Retrieved from The Standard: https://www.standard.co.uk/news/uk/harry-justin-welby-archbishop-windsor-oprah-winfrey-b927152.html

Rajan, A. (2021, December 8). *The Princes and the Press.* Retrieved from BBC2: https://www.bbc.co.uk/programmes/m0011w wf

Rajan, A., & Lee, J. (2021, November 23). *Prince Harry: Private investigator apologises for targeting prince's ex-girlfriend.* Retrieved from BBC News: https://www.bbc.co.uk/news/uk-59361142

Ravikumar, S. (2023, February 9). *British press regulator to investigate Clarkson column on Meghan.* Retrieved from Reuters: https://www.reuters.com/world/uk/british-press-regulator-investigate-clarkson-column-meghan-2023-02-09/

Rayner, G. (2016, November 26). *The Duke of Cambridge approved Prince Harry's plea to trolls to leave Meghan Markle alone.* Retrieved from The Telegraph: https://www.telegraph.co.uk/news/2016/11/

26/duke-cambridge-approved-prince-harrys-
plea-trolls-leave-meghan/

Royal.UK. (2019, January 10). *The Duchess of Sussex
announces Patronages*. Retrieved from Royal
UK: https://www.royal.uk/duchess-sussex-
announces-patronages

Royston, J. (2021, February 10). *Prince Harry and
Meghan Markle Discussed More Negatively
Online Than in Mainstream Media*. Retrieved
from Newsweek:
https://www.newsweek.com/prince-harry-
meghan-markle-discussed-more-negatively-
online-mainstream-media-new-york-time-
1634963

Royston, J. (2022, March 16). *Meghan Markle and Prince
Harry's Three Big Lawsuits So Far This Year*.
Retrieved from Newsweek:
https://www.newsweek.com/meghan-markle-
prince-harry-three-big-lawsuits-this-year-uk-
government-samantha-markle-1688429

Royston, J. (2023, February 13). *How Prince Harry's
Security Lawsuit Could Get More Awkward for
the Royals*. Retrieved from Newsweek:
https://www.newsweek.com/how-prince-
harry-security-lawsuit-could-get-more-
awkward-royal-household-cabinet-1684001

Sabur, R., & Nanu, M. (2023, January 9). *Prince Harry GMA interview: Queen Elizabeth 'never angry' but was 'sad' about Megxit* . Retrieved from The Telegraph: https://www.telegraph.co.uk/royal-family/2023/01/09/prince-harry-gma-interview-live-good-morning-america-interview/

Samuelson, K. (2017, November 27). *A Detailed History of Prince Harry and Meghan Markle's Relationship.* Retrieved from Time: https://time.com/5036452/prince-harry-meghan-markle-relationship-timeline/

Sangster, E. (2023, February). *Meghan Markle seemingly criticises Princess Kate and Prince William's wedding in a resurfaced blog post.* Retrieved from Harper's Bazaar: https://harpersbazaar.com

Shay, J. (2002). *Odysseus In America: Combat Trauma And The Trials Of Homecoming.* New York: Schribner.

Shay, J. (2003). *Achilles in Vietnam: Combat trauma and the undoing of character.* New York: Schribner.

Shay, J. (2014, March). *The Hidden Wounds of War, Keynote address.* Retrieved from Intertexts: Vol.16, No.1 Texas Tech University Press

Sinay, D. (2021, May 17). *Meghan Markle Losing the Name 'Duchess' Would Automatically Get Her a Princess Title Instead.* Retrieved from Yahoo Entertainment: https://www.yahoo.com/entertainment/meghan-markle-losing-name-duchess-163502389.html

Sinek, S. (2017). *Leaders Eat Last: Why Some Teams Pull Together and Others Don't.* Penguin.

Sky-News. (2023, March 28). *Prince Harry: Five things we learned from Duke of Sussex's High Court submission.* Retrieved from Sky News: https://news.sky.com/story/prince-harry-five-things-we-learned-from-duke-of-sussexs-high-court-submission-12844405

Stern, M. (2022, August 18). *John Stevens was tasked with heading the inquiry into Princess Diana's death. He talks to The Daily Beast about the evidence, conspiracy theories, and telling William and Harry.* Retrieved from Daily Beast: https://www.thedailybeast.com/the-man-who-investigated-princess-dianas-death-tells-all

Sussex, H. (2022, December 8). *Harry & Meghan.* Retrieved from Netflix.

Sutin, A. (2007, December 4). *Autobiographical memory as a dynamic process:.* Retrieved from Science

Direct: http://www.self-
definingmemories.com/Sutin_2008.pdf

Swift, J. (2022, July 22). *Duke of Sussex-V-Home
Secretary*. Retrieved from Courts and Tribunals
Judiciary:
https://www.judiciary.uk/judgments/duke-of-
sussex-v-home-secretary/

Sykes, T. (2021, March 10). *Piers Morgan Was Fired
After Meghan Markle Sent an Official Complaint
to His Network*. Retrieved from Daily Beast:
https://news.yahoo.com/piers-morgan-fired-
meghan-markle-130715017.html

Taylor, A. (2021, March 11). *Harry and Meghan: What's
the media's 'invisible contract' with British
royalty?* Retrieved from BBC News:
https://www.bbc.co.uk/news/entertainment-
arts-56326807

Taylor, A. (2021, March 11). *Harry and Meghan: What's
the media's 'invisible contract' with British
royalty?* Retrieved from BBC News:
https://www.bbc.co.uk/news/entertainment-
arts-56326807

Today. (2022, April 20). *Prince Harry Talks Visiting
Queen Elizabeth, Fatherhood In TODAY Exclusive*.
Retrieved from YouTube:

https://www.youtube.com/watch?v=0Lvlv5AY
dZc

Vranic, A., Jelic, M., & Tonkovic, M. (2018, February 27).
*Functions of Autobiographical Memory in
Younger and Older Adults.* Retrieved from
Frontiers:
https://www.frontiersin.org/articles/10.3389/
fpsyg.2018.00219/full

Waterson, J. (2020, January 14). *Meghan legal action:
Mail on Sunday could call Thomas Markle to high
court.* Retrieved from The Guardian:
https://www.theguardian.com/uk-
news/2020/jan/14/mail-on-sunday-could-call-
thomas-markle-in-high-court-defence

Wiki. (2023, February 14). *IMPRESS.* Retrieved from
Wikipedia:
https://en.wikipedia.org/wiki/IMPRESS

Wiki. (2023, February 14). *News International phone
hacking scandal.* Retrieved from Wikipedia:
https://en.wikipedia.org/wiki/News_Internatio
nal_phone_hacking_scandal

Windsor, E. (2017, October 13). *King Edward VIII
Abdication Address.* Retrieved from American
Rhetoric:
https://www.americanrhetoric.com/speeches/
kingedwardVIIIabdication.htm

Wood, V. (2023, January 13). *Prince Harry: 'There's enough for another book – I cut memoir in half to spare my family'*. Retrieved from The Telegraph: https://www.telegraph.co.uk/royal-family/2023/01/13/prince-harry-book-two-spare-revelations-royal-family/

Worthington, E. (2004, September 1). *The New Science of Forgiveness*. Retrieved from Greater Good Magazine: https://greatergood.berkeley.edu/article/item/the_new_science_of_forgiveness

Zisook, S., & Shear, K. (2009). *Grief and Bereavement: What Psychiatrists Need to Know*. Retrieved from NCBI: http://www.ncbi.nlm.nih.gov/pmc/articles/PMC2691160

Printed in Great Britain
by Amazon

22830365R00155